I ♥ MY BOOK

Please Return It!

Mr. & Mrs. F. David Ramsey, Jr.
8305 57th Street West
Tacoma, Washington 98467

EQUALITY and SUBMISSION
in Marriage

EQUALITY
and
SUBMISSION
in Marriage

John C. Howell

BROADMAN PRESS
Nashville, Tennessee

4256–32
ISBN: 0–8054–5632–5

Dewey Decimal Classification: 301.42
Subject heading: MARRIAGE
Library of Congress Catalog Card Number: 78–67292
Printed in the United States of America.

Preface

During the past three years it has been my privilege to lead conferences at the Baptist conference centers in Glorieta, New Mexico, and Ridgecrest, North Carolina, on biblical teachings about marriage and family relationships. In addition, the basic material has also been used in state family conferences and local church family emphases. The creative involvement of the conference participants in discussions and response has helped to clarify the issues and shape the proposed answers. Their continued encouragement to have the material published has led to the writing of this book. I express my appreciation to the hundreds of persons who shared in this venture of exploration.

I also want to express appreciation to the staff in the Family Ministry Department of The Sunday School Board of the Southern Baptist Convention for their interest in helping Christian families apply the teachings of the Bible to daily life in the family. It is my hope that this study will be useful to that task.

Doris, my wife, has worked through the manuscript with me and smoothed out many phrases that might have missed the mark of good communication. In our journey of over thirty years of marriage, we have had to test many of the principles suggested in these pages. I am grateful for her understanding and love in encouraging the writing of the book.

Dedicated to our sons
Michael Christian
and
John Mark
who have helped
us learn the
meaning of family.

Contents

I

Marriage and Family in Biblical Perspective

The roots of Christian teachings about marriage and family go deep into the ancient laws and customs of God's revelation in the Old Testament. The teachings of Jesus and Paul concerning marriage are based firmly on their interpretation of the first two chapters of Genesis. Teachings concerning parent-child relationships are grounded in the Ten Commandments. References to marriage ceremonies practiced in the Old Testament culture are evident in the parables and experiences of Jesus as he lived among the people of Palestine.

One of the valuable contributions of the Old Testament record is that it gives us insight into the failures as well as the successes of families with whom God dealt. The biblical writers were led of God to give us glimpses of family life among the ordinary people of Israel as well as the patriarchs and rulers. We can identify with their humanity as we redeem our own failures by God's grace and rejoice in our own successes through dependence on his Spirit.

In our discussion of Christian marriage and family life, therefore, we will include concepts which had their origin in Hebrew life even though the New Testament may not speak directly to all of the issues involved. Our purpose will always be to separate specific teachings concerning family relationships from the social customs common to the culture of the biblical world. As we evaluate what Christian marriage can be in the twentieth century, we must guard against baptizing the cultural norms of the biblical world rather than letting the gospel of our Lord Jesus Christ free us from the bondage of that culture. The liberating experience of the gospel must always take precedence over the cultural patterns of an ancient time if these patterns deny true personhood to every believer. This approach will be discussed in more detail later in the book.

The purpose of this chapter is to examine briefly the nature of Christian marriage as revealed in the Bible and then to discuss the importance of the family in Hebrew-Christian life.

The Nature of Christian Marriage

There are many ways in which this topic might be discussed. In my book *Growing in Oneness* I described Christian marriages as a relationship of commitment, communion, and consummation. However, since we are concerned in this chapter with marriage as a social reality as well as a spiritual relationship, we will use a different analysis of the nature of Christian marriage. The key words here will be *contract, covenant,* and *commitment.*

Social Contract

Christian marriage is a social contract. One definition of the word *contract* is the act by which two parties enter into a marriage relation or into the agreement to do so demonstrated by engagement. To enter into a contract includes the assumption of legal accountability or responsibility for the argreement made between two or more persons. In ancient and contemporary law, marriage is a contract which involves legal contractual responsibilities.

But it is also true that marriage is a social reality. Sociologists study marriages and family life. Social customs as well as laws influence the way in which a marriage is established. Religious rites and celebrations have developed over the centuries which demonstrate the impact of society on the social reality of the family. One distinguishing characteristic of Christian marriage is the social contract into which the participants enter by marrying. Thus in *The New English Bible* translation of Matthew 1:19, Joseph is described as desiring "to have the marriage contract set aside quietly" when he discovered Mary to be pregnant.[1]

It is a *contract between families* (Gen. 24:1–67; Ruth). The biblical world, especially in Old Testament culture, was a family-centered one. An individual really did not exist as a separate person apart from his identification with the family unit. The family even bore a collective responsibility for righteousness and for sin in the lives of individual family members (Josh. 7:1–26). In this type of family situation, the father exercised almost absolute power over the lives and affairs of his wife and children. He was truly the patriarch of the home.

Since a son's wife became a member of his father's household, it was customary for the father to choose a wife for his son. Sometimes he entrusted this responsibility to a loyal servant who would commit himself to carrying out his master's wishes. In either case, the marriage arrangements were established as a contract between the families of the bride and groom.

Genesis 24:1–67 records a clear example of marriage as a contract between families. When it was time for Isaac to marry, Abraham's advanced age made it impossible for him to journey back to the land of his fathers to personally select the bride. He charged Eliezer, his oldest servant, with the responsibility of going to Mesopotamia to choose a wife for Isaac. After Eliezer was led to the right woman, he negotiated a contract with her father, Bethuel, and her brother, Laban. When they were satisfied with the arrangement, Bethuel and Laban declared, "Behold, Rebekah is before you, take her and go, and let her be the wife of your master's son, as the Lord has spoken" (24:51).[2]

In token of the completion of the contract, "the servant brought forth jewelry of silver and of gold, and raiment, and gave them to Rebekah; he also gave to her brother and to her mother costly ornaments" (24:53). These gifts may have been part of the bride price which Abraham would pay to Rebekah's family. Since he sent ten camels loaded with gifts (24:10), Abraham demonstrated his high position among the people of the land. Payment of a large bride price considerably increased the prestige of the bridegroom and his father!

All of this sounds strangely old-fashioned when we realize that many modern marriages occur in which one partner may not even meet the parents of the mate until the wedding rehearsal! It would be futile to propose that Christians revive the family contract as a basis for getting married since this would never work in our mobile society. It is important, however, for Christian couples to recognize the value of parental acceptance of their marriage in developing a strong family relationship.

The young girl in a premarital counseling session who blurted out, "I'm marrying him, not his family!" was only partially correct. In one sense she marries his family even if she never meets them. Her husband's understanding of and his attitude toward marriage was largely shaped by his experience of living in a family as he grew up in his own home. By knowing how he related to his parents, and especially to his mother, she could gain insight into the way he might develop his relationship with her.

In addition, marital research demonstrates that couples who have mutually good relationships with the parents of their mates tend to have better marriages. Parental support expressed in many friendly ways can help a marriage get started well and give it a warmth of friendship that is rewarding.

While writing this portion of the book, I attended a wedding which symbolized the happiness of mutual family support. The fathers of the bride and groom were both ministers and shared equally in performing the wedding ceremony. The groom's father led the bride in her vows while the bride's father led the groom in his affirmations. The two fathers pronounced the couple as husband and wife in unison. The entire experience gave eloquent testimony of the joyful acceptance of this marriage by the families of the radiant young couple. Through the marriage the two families were brought into a new and meaningful relationship.

For some couples, however, the awareness of this mutuality of involvement in new family patterns may not be felt so keenly until children are born. Suddenly the parents of the couple become grandparents! The dynamics of family living are apt to change with the impact of this significant event. Vacation trips must now include visits to grandma and grandpa in order that grandparent and grandchild may have opportunity to share the drama of family continuity that stretches back through time. Competitive claims on such visits may introduce new tensions in the young marriage, but the joys of the relationship may also increase.

So the family contract is out for contemporary Christian marriage, but the importance of good family contacts is not! The social reality of marriage includes its tie to the past through one's family, and this reality must be nurtured in marriage today. Perhaps the success of Alex Haley's novel *Roots* in awakening a sensitivity to one's heritage may also symbolize the desire for closer family ties across generational lines.

Christian marriage is also a *contract between persons* (Gen. 24:57–58,67; 29:15–21). Often the father in Old Testament times arranged his daughter's marriage without asking her consent. This can be seen in Jacob's deal with Laban (Gen. 29:15–21) when Leah and Rachel seemingly had no choice in becoming wives of Jacob. In some cases, though, the daughter was allowed to express her decision about the choice. Such was the experience of Rebekah as recorded in Genesis 24:57–58. After Eliezer had completed his negotiations, Bethuel and Laban said, " 'We will call the maiden, and ask her.' And they called Rebekah, and said to her, 'Will you go with this man?' She said, 'I will go.' " The marriage became her personal contract as well as a family contract.

To say that marriage is a social contract between persons highlights the importance of responsibility or accountability in human relationships. During the 1960s and early 1970s, many young people decided they would live together for love without accepting society's demand for a license and ceremony creating a legal marriage. Their emphasis on the importance of love in marriage is commendable and has fundamental biblical support. There is no more beautiful love story in the Bible than that of Jacob's desire for Rachel to be his wife (Gen. 29:9–30). Because of his love for her, Jacob committed himself to Laban, her father, for seven years of work as a bride price. The biblical writer comments, "Jacob served seven years for Rachel, and they seemed to him but a few days because of the love he had for her" (29:30). Even though Laban tricked him into marrying Leah first, Jacob's love for Rachel was the basis for the marriage they later shared.

In their emphasis on love, however, these young people have focused primarily on love as "good feelings" while neglecting love as ethical responsibility for the consequences of the relationship. It is of course true that common-law marriage without benefit of license or ceremony can have legal standing in the eyes of the state when the couple live together out of their desire to be responsible to and for one another. It is not this type of relationship with which we are concerned if that assumption of responsibility is real. Our concern is for the couples who reject the right of state or society to have any stake in their relationship since their love is a private and not a social event. Is this really true, especially for Christians?

Historically the Christian faith did not develop a theology of the wedding ceremony until it became a sacrament in the Roman Catholic Church. The churches were concerned that the marriage express proper responsibility. Thus Christians were always more concerned about persons than about ceremonies and documents.

If this be true, why should churches today be upset when

couples declare that they are marrying each other and do not need any license or ceremony to make their marriage official?

The answer to this question lies in the social aspect of marriage. Christians in the confused moralities of the New Testament world were expected to obey the laws of the state "for the sake of conscience" (Rom. 13:5) and "for the Lord's sake" (1 Pet. 2:13). Their obedience was necessary to uphold the social fabric of life because they were part of that social reality. In similar manner today the Christian's willingness to be obedient to the laws of society helps strengthen the social fabric of American life. Joseph Hough has expressed this idea well in his article on "Rules and the Ethics of Sex." Hough points out that "no act on the part of any two persons can be isolated from the social nexus." He describes what this means by saying:

True humanity is social, and as such it involves the obligation not only to be human in interpersonal relationships but also to honor those structures by which we try to provide the possibility for true humanity by protecting each other from the abuses that result from immoral actions.[3]

Marriage is thus "the social sign of the truly human relationship that must be the moral context for sexual intercourse." Through participation in a legal marriage ceremony, whether civil or religious, the Christian couple affirm their willingness to uphold the social good of the community in which they live as husband and wife.

Another aspect of this social emphasis is the willingness to accept legal as well as emotional responsibility for the persons in the relationship and for children who may be born into the relationship. It is impossible for the couple to know ahead of time what kinds of emotional, physical, or financial problems they may confront in developing their relationship. Marriage provides them with a framework of commitment within which to work out these differences. Merely living together without this openly expressed commitment makes it easy for one person to move out of the relationship to protect himself regardless of the hurt inflicted on the other. As Hough put it, the couple are in effect saying: "Not only are we emotionally tied to each other, but the evidence of our good faith is that we want the world to share in the knowledge of our life together and to hold us responsible within our common social existence for the vows we make to each other."[4] This is certainly one indication that Christian love as *agape* exists within the relationship. It is the love that bears responsibility for and accountability to all that takes place in the developing life of the family. It is essential to the fullest sense of Christian responsibility in the personal and social reality of life together. This is what we mean by saying that Christian marriage is a contract between the persons involved in it.

But Christian marriage is more than a social contract—it is also a spiritual covenant.

Spiritual Covenant

The concept of covenant is basic to one's understanding of God's relationship with his people. In the Old Testament the glory and the shame of Israel are directly related to the nation's obedience or disobedience to the covenant established by themselves and God.

The writer of Deuteronomy reminded the people that God "declared to you his covenant, which he commanded you to perform, that is, the ten commandments; and he wrote them upon two tables of stone" (4:13). Then he warned them, "Take heed to yourselves, lest you forget the covenant of the Lord your God, which he made with you" (4:23). This covenant was a relationship of blessing based upon obedience to the revealed word of the living God.

In later days when Israel had failed so often to remain obedient in love, God declared through Jeremiah:

Behold, the days are coming, says the Lord, when I will make a new covenant with the house of Israel and the house of Judah, not like the convenant which I made with their fathers when I took them by the hand to bring them out of the land of Egypt, my convenant which they broke, though I was their husband, says the Lord. But this is the covenant which I will make with the house of Israel after those days, says the Lord: I will put my law within them, and I will write it upon their hearts; and I will be their God, and they shall be my people (Jer. 31:31–33).

Notice in this passage that the covenant relationship is described as between the wife or bride and her husband. It is a covenant of love and response, but Israel broke the covenant by her spiritual unfaithfulness. Then God promises to establish an even more personal covenant—one that will be heartfelt and intimate. This new covenant in biblical history is fulfilled in Jesus Christ. Remember his inspiring words at the Last Supper as the cup of wine was given to his disciples: "Drink of it, all of you; for this is my blood of the covenant, which is poured out for many for the forgiveness of sins" (Matt. 26:27–28).

Thus the spiritual covenant is to be one's personal response to and acceptance of the mate in a relationship characterized by mutual love, expressed forgiveness, and a shared faith.

The prophet Malachi is clear in his description of marriage as a covenant. While many churchmen do not know that Malachi said anything except, "bring the full tithes into the storehouse" (3:10), he is as emphatic in his condemnation of unfaithfulness to the covenant marriage as he is in condemning unfaithfulness to the covenant between God and his people (2:10–16). His understanding of covenant seems to be twofold; the personal covenant between husband and wife, and the covenant relationship of Israel within which the marriage was consummated. Thus his concept of the meaning of covenant is similar to Jeremiah.

In Malachi's time the Jewish men were evidently divorcing the wives whom they married when both were young and were now marrying younger women out of the pagan people among whom they lived. Malachi declared God's judgment on this practice because "the Lord was witness to the covenant between you and the wife of your youth, to whom you have been faithless, though she is your companion and your wife by covenant" (2:14). They had been married within the covenant of faith and on the basis of a covenant of commitment.

How can contemporary Christian marriages fulfill the covenant concept as described in these Old Testament experiences? *Christians can enter into marriages with those who share their basic commitment to the Christian faith* as a vital foundation for the covenant life of marriage. The person who has discovered a new selfhood in Jesus Christ gains courage to share himself with another person and is thus able to develop trust by being willing to love freely. In John's beautiful and powerful words, "There is no fear in love, but perfect love casts out fear" (1 John 4:18).

Having the wedding ceremony in the church becomes one way of affirming the marriage vows as personal expressions of covenant which also celebrate the covenant of faith within which the couple live. As the wedding ritual expresses it, "We are gathered together in the sight of God and this assembly to join together this man and this woman in the holy estate of matrimony." This covenant of faith is foundational to Christian marriage even though couples without shared faith can and do experience good marriages. To have a common faith provides a perspective from which to view joys and sorrows, victories and defeats. It is the integrating force making clear the ultimate loyalties and mutual concerns of life. Giving meaning to life, it looks beyond the limited horizons of human existence to see God's ultimate redemption of their love.

Christians can make their marriage vows be personal declarations of self-giving rather than rituals prescribed by social custom. Even though the context is one of friendship rather than marriage, the covenant of Jonathan and David symbolizes the type of self-giving needed in the marriage covenant. The Bible records, that "the soul of Jonathan was knit to the soul of David, and Jonathan loved him as his own soul . . . . Then Jonathan made a covenant with David, because he loved him as his own soul" (1 Sam. 18:1,3). Marriage as a covenant requires the kind of self-giving in which the two persons unselfishly care for one another, and the marital vows affirm this.

One of the encouraging aspects of modern marriage is the desire of Christian couples to write their own vows. In this way the affirmations made to each other are heartfelt expressions of their personal covenant witnessed by the friends assembled at the wedding. In one recent wedding the bride and groom faced each other as they held hands and then spoke freely of their personal commitment to one another. It was a moving and truly Christian confirmation of their covenant of marriage.

All couples may not be able to write their own vows or have confidence enough to attempt an uncoached speech at a time such as this! But every couple can let their vows be honest declarations of faithfulness to the one-flesh union being established in their marriage.

The spiritual covenant is both communal and personal. In both aspects it depends largely on the personal commitment which the couple make to one another. It is also true that commitment as well as covenant is essential to maintaining marriage as a social contract.

Samuel Southard relates the experience of a friend who said she discovered the importance of marriage as a social contract involving commitment only after two years of marriage. During the first year she thought all was bliss. In the second year she found some parts of marriage boring. But in the routine of married life, she was learning to make adjustments and find satisfaction in the relationship. She declared that working it out was easier because she had made a commitment to this man before many witnesses, and it was up to the two of them to work it out. So marriage, in addition to being contract and covenant, is also commitment.

Personal Commitment

Although the word *commitment* is not a biblical word, the concept is fundamentally so. At times the idea is expressed as "stedfastness" or "loyalty," while at other times it is included in "righteousness" as a quality of relationship.

For a number of years the younger generation of Americans were exposed to books and teachings which made light of or rejected completely the idea of personal commitment to marriage. All relationships were expendable. Change was inevitable, and relationships were fractured by the ever-increasing rate of change. Commitment was not only unnecessary but it could also increase the possibility of personal unhappiness in a mobile, changing society.

Now, however, there seems to be a new emphasis on the vital place of commitment in marriage if personal fulfillment is to occur. We could say the contemporary society is rediscovering what the Bible described centuries ago: " 'It is not good that the man should be alone; I will make him a helper fit for him.' . . . Therefore a man leaves his father and his mother and cleaves to his wife, and they become one flesh" (Gen. 2:18,24). This is the essence of commitment.

Let us examine three aspects of commitment in the marriage relationship.

First, *marriage involves a commitment to mutual need fulfillment.* People marry because of need for another person in some way. They discover for themselves that it is not good to be alone, and they find someone who will share life in the intimacy of a marital experience. Obviously one person is not always aware of the basic needs which impel him to marriage, so we often cloak our basic desire for need fulfillment under the cover word, *love!*

The Howard Clinebells are absolutely right, however, when they declare that "intimacy is not so much a matter of what or how much is shared as it is *the degree of mutual need-satis-*

faction within the relationship."[5] When couples are able to understand and communicate their basic needs to mates who can accept and develop ways to meet those mutual needs in their commitment to become one flesh, then marital intimacy · will grow.

One note of warning needs to be sounded at this point, however. Since need fulfillment has become so dominant in modern society, it is possible for a man or woman to destroy an otherwise good marriage because expectations for need satisfaction are too extreme. The needs themselves may be so neurotic that no relationship could ever satisfy them. In situations like this, persons can literally be consumed by their mates' expectations or the person with neurotic needs will go from one disillusioning experience to another. Such persons need professional counseling to better cope with the excessive nature of their emotional needs.

Second, *marriage involves a commitment to a continuing relationship.* In the Christian understanding, marriage is to last! This type of commitment may seem naive when we realize that a million or more marriages are dissolved by divorce, dissolution, or annulment every year. However, to approach marriage with a fingers-crossed attitude is to deny the essential meaning of the one-flesh relationship. In Jesus' response to the argument over divorce recorded in Matthew 19 and Mark 10, he was unequivocal in his affirmation that marriage was to last.

It is appropriate to consider the close tie between this kind of commitment and the building of a strong relationship. George and Nena O'Neill, in their book *Open Marriage,* described marriage in such a way that commitment seemed to be detrimental to the relationship. In their later book, *Shifting Gears,* they deliberately and clearly discussed the importance of commitment. They said, *"Relationship* is the essence of commitment and through working at this relationship we give and extend ourselves; learn and grow. Commitment means accept-

ing the limitations—routine, materials, hours, personality—
both of ourselves and of the other we are committed to."[6]
While the O'Neill's probably would not adopt the same analogy,
this statement reflects very concisely the philosophy that Paul
set forth when he said, "Forbearing one another in love," and
"speaking the truth in love, we are to grow up in every way
into him who is the head, into Christ" (Eph. 4:2,15).

Many couples have discovered the true meaning of their
love only after their basic commitment to a continuing relationship brought them through some difficult times of marital adjustment. Even though this does not mean that *every* marriage
can survive or even should survive, it does mean that the commitment to work things out may keep the couple together
long enough to grow up into being lovers more realistically.

Third, *marriage is a commitment to fulfilling role relationships.* There is probably more intensive controversy going
on today concerning appropriate roles for men and women
than at any other time in recent Christian history. The whole
male/female issue will be discussed in the following chapters,
but at this point the need for compatible role relationships
in a growing marriage must be made clear.

The idea of role in marriage involves the behavioral expectations which men and women have for themselves and for their
mates when they marry. These expectations have been shaped
by the way parents functioned at home, by the teachings received from church and other religious sources, by the common
expectations discussed among peer groups, and by television
images of family life. The influence of family and peers is most
pronounced in forming role expectations.

Since the husband and wife have usually grown up in different environments, different expectations can create the first
arguments in a marriage. If these early conflicts are not solved
through understanding and acceptance, as well as change when
necessary, the role conflict problem may continue to haunt
the relationship.

For happily married couples there is usually a growing sense of harmony between expectation and reality, especially with regard to methods of dealing with arguments and conflicts. A basic commitment to developing fulfilling role behaviors is vital to such a union.

Christian marriage is therefore a blending of social contract, spiritual covenant, and personal commitment. It involves the family of origin and the family of faith. It requires love, forgiveness, and growth. It is one of the most demanding, exasperating, fulfilling, and exciting adventures of life. It is God's way for human fulfillment when his will is being done. Marriage is also the foundation of the family. Let us now look briefly at the importance of the family in Christian perspective.

The Importance of the Family

In the December, 1977, issue of *Ladies Home Journal,* noted author James A. Michener has an article on the future of the American family. One of his interesting conclusions is that "the form a family takes depends in large part upon the psychological mood of the nations within which it functions."[7] Through his intensive study of American social history, Michener suggests that the family formed a basic core of human life from Pilgrim days through the period immediately preceding World War II. But after the war, we entered a period of continual assault on the family from educators, as well as plain people on every hand.

What of today? Michener expresses the hope that the tide may be turning, that a national consensus may be developing which will insist upon the preservation and protection of the family. The proposed White House Conference of Families is one tangible expression of the government's concern in this area.

Michener observes that "people live best when they live in mutually supportive units, and the best so far devised is a family."[8] If the national mood truly does affect the attitude toward families, as Michener maintains, then our nation could well adopt much of the positive mood toward families revealed in the Bible.

The command to bear children is given to human life as a blessing to be experienced in God's purpose for existence. In the words of the ancient writer, "God blessed them, and God said to them, 'Be fruitful and multiply, and fill the earth and subdue it' " (Gen. 1:28). The original pair were to find joyous fulfillment of their one-flesh relationship in childbirth and family life.

Throughout the Old Testament *the family is fundamental to human growth.* Property rights and inheritance laws were by families. For example, in the settling of the land of Canaan, the land was to be divided "by lot according to your families" (Num. 33:54). Family lineage was basic to a person's place in the community, thus the Bible contains the long genealogies that trace a family's existence through many generations (compare Ex. 6; Num. 25; and Matt. 1).

Worship also was a family experience. The annual observance of the Passover was a family ritual presided over by the father (Ex. 13:3–20). Parents were commanded to love their Lord and to teach the children through household ritual the ways of faith (Deut. 6:4–9). Until the development of the synagogue during the postexilic and interbiblical periods, families went to the Temple only a few times during the year and worshiped at home the rest of the time.

The New Testament has many suggestive insights into the family as the developer of faith. The home into which Jesus was born was deeply religious as shown in the strict obedience of Mary and Joseph to the Law (Luke 2:21–24,39–41). Jesus' own growing life was shaped by obedience to his home teachings (Luke 2:51–52).

Paul's commendation of Timothy attributes the young preacher's faith to the influence of family. Paul said, "I am reminded of your sincere faith, a faith that dwelt first in your grandmother Lois and your mother Eunice and now, I am sure, dwells in you" (2 Tim. 1:5).

Someone has suggested that Paul described the family as "a school of life." In his letters he encouraged older women to teach younger women how to fulfill their role as wives and mothers. Older men are encouraged to be a proper example for young men, and children are to honor their parents. The home is thus a Christian training center to equip believers for life in relationship with each other and with the society in which they live.

Contemporary sociologists and psychologists certainly agree that the family is a school for living. As Christian families we have the opportunity, responsibility, and challenge of creating homes providing models for healthy, happy family life in our world. The importance of such a family cannot be overstated.

The remaining chapters of this book will focus on the interrelationships of family members. My desire is to help couples experience joy in their marriage and fulfillment in their families through personal response to the gospel of love and freedom in Jesus Christ. Too many Christians live unhappily in marriage patterns which inhibit their own sense of the new life in the Spirit. They are afraid to trust their own sense of what a marriage and family *can be* because of what others have told them it *must be.* As you read, let God's Spirit truly guide you into the abundant life of marriage and family relationships that will honor Christ by fulfilling his new life in you.

Notes

1. Copyright © The Delegates of the Oxford University Press and the Syndics of the Cambridge University Press, 1961, 1970. Reprinted by permission. Subsequent quotations are marked (NEB).

2. Unless otherwise indicated, Scripture quotations are from the Re-

vised Standard Version of the Bible, copyrighted 1946, 1952, © 1971, 1973 by the Division of Christian Education of the National Council of Churches of Christ in the U.S.A., and used by permission.

3. Joseph C. Hough, Jr., "Rules and Ethics of Sex," *Moral Issues and Christian Response*, eds. Paul T. Jersild and Dale A. Johnson, 2nd ed. (New York: Holt, Rinehart and Winston, 1976), pp. 98–99.

4. Ibid., p. 99.

5. Howard J. and Charlotte H. Clinebell, *The Intimate Marriage* (New York: Harper and Row, 1970), p. 1.

6. George and Nena O'Neill, *Shifting Gears* (New York: Avon Books, 1975), p. 185.

7. James A. Michener, "The American Family," *Ladies Home Journal* (December, 1977), p. 116.

8. Ibid.

II

The Persons in Marriage

One of the definitions given in *Webster's New International Dictionary* for the word *person* is "the real self of a human being." In our discussion of persons in a marriage, this definition clearly defines what we want to consider: Two real people of equal value can create a relationship in love in which intimacy may grow into oneness.

This objective raises some interesting and paradoxical questions. How can equality and yieldedness be maintained in the same relationship? How are individual selfhood and a growing oneness between the two persons to be kept in balance? What is the meaning of *intimacy?* Is this purpose true to God's intentional will for marriage?

Other questions will undoubtedly come to your mind as you read, but let us begin to discuss the nature of personhood and its importance in Christian marriage.

Created Male/Female

Within the exciting first chapters of Genesis, the biblical writers establish clearly the foundation of human personhood in God's creative activity: *Man is created in God's image.* The symbolism of the text captures the highest acclaim that can be given to human life when it says, "So God created man in his own image, in the image of God he created him; male and female he created them . . . . And God saw everything that he had made, and behold, it was very good" (Gen. 1:27,31). In a later passage, the Bible sums up this creation of man and woman in its affirmation that "when God created man, he made him in the likeness of God. Male and female he created them, and he blessed them and named them Man when they were created" (Gen. 5:1–2).

Many of the religions of the ancient past, as well as the modern present, attempted to portray God in terms of man's nature. At times even the Hebrews described God in terms of man's own way of acting out his feelings toward others. But the heart of Old Testament teaching in the Law and in the Prophets continually sets before human beings the challenge to become like their God rather than allow God to become man intensified. For example, the "holiness code" of Leviticus established the highest ethical standard possible when the Scripture records, "Say to the people of Israel, I am the Lord your God . . . . You shall be holy; for I the Lord your God am holy" (Lev. 18:1; 19:1).

Notice, however, that man who bears the image and likeness of God is not simply male, but male and female. The equality of persons in this tremendous interpretation of the origins of life is clearly established. Even though there is a strong reaction evident in our land to sexist language, the word translated "man" in this passage is the generic term referring to all human beings. All mankind bears the image of the Creator even though that image has been affected deeply by human sin.

When Jesus was confronted with a test question concerning his own position on divorce, Jesus refused to be drawn into the current debate on reasons for divorce. Instead he reminded his questioners of God's original purpose for marriage as the establishment of a one-flesh union between persons who had been created as male and female in the beginning (Matt. 19:4–6; Mark 10:6). Jesus very emphatically emphasized the male-female relationship as God's purpose for life.

Paul K. Jewett, professor of systematic theology at Fuller Theological Seminary in California, has written a provocative treatment of maleness/femaleness in the context of Genesis

1 and 2. He declares that the essential nature of man as male/female is what truly reflects God's image in us. Rather than focusing on reason, spiritual sensitivity, and personality as the basic elements of the image of God in human life, Jewett follows Karl Barth in maintaining that "to be in the image of God *is* to be male and female. Not only do men and women alike participate in the divine image, but their fellowship as male and female is what it *means* to be in the image of God."[1] His book *Man as Male and Female* has been greeted with acclaim as well as rejection by Christian theologians, but I am in accord with his basic thesis that the equality of personhood for man and woman is clearly described in the creation narratives. In spite of man's failure to fulfill God's will in the story of the Fall, the Old Testament sets forth a continual enhancement of the integrity of personhood. In Jesus' teachings the value of persons as possessing worth by God's creative act becomes central to his concern for people. Personhood rests upon the image of God in man by creation and upon the recreation of life in Christ through faith in God's revelation of love at the cross.

Male/female is reflected in biological distinctiveness. It all seems so very simple. The doctor checks out the physical appearance of the newborn and then announces to the mother or father, "It's a boy" or "It's a girl." The ancient purpose of God for human life is once again affirmed by the maleness or femaleness of the body structure. Conception to birth has been fulfilled once more in an uncomplicated and direct way.

Yet contemporary research in human sexuality has shown us how complicated the pathway really is from that moment when an ovum is fertilized by a probing sperm deep in the woman's body to the final drama of birth. John Money and Patricia Tucker point out that the way from conception to birth is not two roads unerringly pointed toward male or female but "one road with a number of forks where each of us turns in either the male or the female direction. You become male or female by stages."[2] Fortunately, most of us turn properly and smoothly in the same direction at each fork and thus are born with a clear sense of our sexual identity. The union of XX chromosomes has resulted in our femaleness; whereas, the union of XY chromosomes has resulted in our maleness. We have therefore a strong appreciation for being male or female.

Money and Tucker call this sexual identity our "gender identity." This is your understanding of yourself as a male or female, the inner acceptance of your biological heritage. This acceptance is vital to your personhood "because your sense of yourself as you, a unique individual—your identity—is the essence of you, and at the core of it lies your sense of yourself as male or female, your gender identity."[3] When God destined man to be male and female, the determinant aspect of the human person was firmly established. Maleness/femaleness laid the groundwork for becoming masculine or feminine.

Man possesses potential for masculine/feminine identification. Masculinity and femininity are based upon biological distinctiveness, but they are not inherently determined simply by being male or female. Instead, these concepts are learned responses to the culture in which we grow up. Male and female refer to our gender identity (XX or XY) but masculine and feminine refer to the ways in which a particular culture defines how each sex should behave in society.

Researchers in family sociology and human sexuality describe this public or social definition of what men and women are to be and do as our gender role. As we have said, roles are primarily definitions of expected behavior taught by one's particular culture. As such they are subject to change as the culture changes. Roles are not established by divine decree in creation in the way that our gender identity is established.

Think for a moment how early we begin socializing our children into the expectations of our society. If the doctor announces that our baby is a boy, we choose blue blankets for the crib! If it is a girl, pink must be the color! From the very moment of birth, we begin to program our thinking and the attitudes of our child into accepted definitions of what it means to be masculine or feminine.

Obviously it is important for each child to develop a healthy sense of femininity or masculinity. To fail to do so can contribute to an inadequate sense of personhood. Our problem is that we often try to identify cultural patterns of another society as the evidence of God's universal intent for all peoples of all cultures. This is to confuse our own understanding of masculine or feminine because we are not free to separate what God intends for us to be in our own time from the culture into which the Word originally came. I agree with the observation by Money and Tucker that "the tendency of cultural stereotypes to resist change is essential for maintaining a society, but flexibility is essential to maintain both the society and its members in health."[4]

Being created (or born) male or female and being happy in our gender identity enables us to adapt old roles and adopt new roles in fulfilling our own understanding of what it means to be masculine or feminine. This understanding will help us feel comfortable with our own sexuality and with the people who become part of our life experience.

Designed to Complement Each Other

The word *complement* is defined as that which fills up or completes by bringing together two mutually completing parts. Each one needs the other to establish completeness. Male and female are designed physically and emotionally to complement each other in establishing a new completeness in life.

This need for complementarity is delightfully described in the second chapter of Genesis. God had created Adam and placed him in the Garden where he could have every physical need supplied.

But something (or someone) was missing,
And Adam was lonely.
So God said, "It is not good for the
    man to be alone,"
And then God created another person,
One who was like Adam
Yet so different.
When Adam saw her, his heart was glad,
And his lips offered praise to God.
So Adam joined his life to hers
And they became one flesh.

The interpretive account of the beginning of female/male relationships recorded in Genesis 2:18–24 is basic to Jesus' interpretation of marriage (Matt. 19:5–6; Mark 10:7–9). The enduring quality of the one-flesh union consummated in the marital union was to be strengthened, not weakened, in the growth of a marriage.

Let us now consider four ways in which the male and female are to complement each other.

They complement each other *in the mutual awareness of their sexuality.* When Adam saw this new creation of God, he exclaimed, "She shall be called woman." She was not another man, and Adam had no difficulty recognizing the difference! After all, they were both naked and were not ashamed (Gen. 2:25). In every culture known to man, the sexuality of male/female dominates the relationship between the sexes.

To interpret sexuality as referring only to the genital contacts between male/female is an inadequate understanding of what is meant. The word or concept actually includes all that we are, physically and emotionally, as male and female. In *Human Sexuality,* a study commissioned by the Catholic Theological Society of America, there is an excellent discussion of the meaning of this term.

Human sexuality is defined as "the concrete manifestation

of the divine call to completion, a call extended to every person in the very act of creation and rooted in the very core of his or her being." The authors point out that "men and women, at every moment of life and in every aspect of living, experience themselves, others, and indeed the whole world in a distinctly male or female way."[5]

Contrary to the unisex movement which seeks to obliterate the differences between male/female, the Christian faith recognizes the differences and emphasizes the complementarity of one to the other. A person of either sex grows into the wholeness of selfhood by fulfilling his own gender identity as male or female because wholeness is independent of sexual union. If this were not so, then Jesus could not be considered a fully whole human being. The Christian's experience of selfhood is not dependent on marriage, but it is dependent on personal faith in Christ. Wholeness as a sexual person is to accept and rejoice in one's maleness or femaleness and to relate to the opposite sex in full awareness of our complementary human sexuality.

Jewett focuses on this basic theme of human interaction when he affirms that "while marriage is perhaps the most intimate form of human fellowship, it is not the most basic. Men and women *become* related as husband and wife, and many do; but they *are* related as men and women by virtue of God's creative act."[6] In a generation when many young adults are delaying marriage until the middle to late 20s, we must affirm their wholeness as persons even before they enter marriage. They relate to each other as male/female in the complementarity built into their lives by the establishment of their gender identity. This joy in one's sexuality does not require sexual union to exist since it is a more basic emotion of self-acceptance. However, the built-in complementarity does establish the setting for sexual union as well as the other ways in which male/female complement each other.

They complement each other *in the personal partnership*

of marriage (Gen. 2:18; 1 Pet. 3:7). The King James Version
of the Bible translates God's purpose in creating woman as
providing a "helpmeet" for Adam. In the Revised Standard
Version she is to be a "helper fit for him." Each of these translations suggests that woman is designed solely to meet the needs
of man.

In *A Christian Theology of the Old Testament,* George
Knight gives us insight into a better understanding of the Hebrew terms used here. He says, "The word 'helpmeet' . . . is
a mistranslation of the original Hebrew. Eve is Adam's . . .
help, corresponding to him. Eve thus complements Adam, just
as Adam complements Eve, with the result that it is the two
together, man and woman, who form what the priestly writer
has called by the name of Adam (Gen. 5:12)."[7] *Today's English
Version* incorporates this meaning of the Hebrew terms when
woman is identified as man's "suitable companion."[8]

To be partners or companions in marriage is to be equal
in personhood. There is no hint in the creation accounts of
Genesis 1 and 2 that woman is subordinate to man. Rather
they share equally in the creating of the partnership. This partnership was affected by sin, as we shall discuss shortly, but
even in the New Testament there are indications that such
partnership is expected.

Paul's discussion of sexual responsibility in Christian marriage
certainly makes the couple equal in their relationship to each
other's needs (1 Cor. 7:3-5). Peter holds to the concept of
woman's physical weakness as indicating the weaker sex, but
he declares that man and woman are joint heirs or partners
in the grace of life that comes through Christ (1 Pet. 3:7).

A poet has captured the joy of complementing each other
in the partnership of marriage in these lines: "With such a
comrade, such a friend/I fain would walk till journey's end."[9]

They complement each other *in sexual union* (Gen. 2:24;
1 Cor. 7:3-5). The biblical writer added his postscript to the
story of woman's creation: "A man leaves his father and his

mother and cleaves to his wife, and they become one flesh" (Gen. 2:24). To become "one flesh" in the early biblical usage of the term was to engage in sexual intercourse and thus consummate the marriage. For example, when Rebekah's marriage to Isaac is described in the Bible, it reads: "Then Isaac brought her into the tent, and took Rebekah, and she became his wife; and he loved her" (Gen. 24:67). The sexual act of becoming one flesh is involved in his bringing her into the tent and taking her.

Since maleness/femaleness are identified by our sexuality in God's purpose, how fitting it is that the sexual union is the most appropriate and joyous way of demonstrating our physical complementarity, also in God's purpose! It was never God's plan that Christianity fall prey to the tragic misinterpretation of sexual experience which identified it with sin. The Bible clearly condemns the misuse of sex in ways that destroy relationships. However, the sexual union is also described as delight and joy in many biblical passages (Prov. 5:18–19; Song of Solomon).

In biblical thought the real self and the body are one with each other. Therefore sexual union is a union not merely of two bodies but of two persons. The body represents the self or the person in this symbolic way.

Sexual experience, the "one flesh" union of husband and wife, is thus another aspect of God's purpose in the complementarity of male and female.

They complement each other *in emotional intimacy* (Gen. 2:24; Matt. 19:5–6). Of all the expectations created in modern America for marriage to fulfill, the desire for intimacy is certainly at the top of the list or close to it. *Intimacy,* in our use of the term, refers to a depth relationship between persons which encourages the recognition of and response to the felt needs of each other. Different couples will experience intimacy in different ways, and all couples will find that intimacy has a rhythm of ebb and flow in the routineness of living.

Genuine intimacy is built upon an acceptance of the authentic personhood of one another as equals in worth. It seems true that such intimacy as we have described cannot take place in a superior-inferior relationship. But even between equals, intimacy is a growing quality of relationship which must be nurtured through ecstasy and conflict in marital life.

I am suggesting that intimacy such as this is implied in the developed meaning of the one-flesh relationship. Already I have pointed to the sexual connotation of this term. Now I want to go a step further to declare that the qualities which sustain intimacy are inferred in the meaning of one flesh.

When Matthew and Mark recorded the account of Jesus' conflict with the Pharisees over divorce, they both captured his basic reference to marriage as a one-flesh relationship (Matt. 19:5–6; Mark 10:7–9). The word translated "one" has the meaning of "one only" or "unique." "Flesh" is more than the material element of the body—it is a symbol of the whole person in this usage of the term. Thus Jesus affirmed that in marriage a woman and a man may complement each other through the creation of a union which uniquely blends their two persons into a new unity.

This oneness does not expect nor demand the absorption of one personality into another. Some people seem to believe this is what oneness means. A man in North Carolina humorously identified the struggle through which many couples go when he said, "For the first five years of our marriage my wife and I struggled to become one. Our problem was that we could not decide which one to become!" Oneness in the concept of one flesh is the potential for intimacy in which personhood is respected and commitment is affirmed.

Howard and Charlotte Clinebell, in their excellent book, *The Intimate Marriage,* describe some of the qualities in marriage which help intimacy grow.[10] The willingness to risk greater openness by being real in the relationship, to be emotionally present to each other, to develop a great degree of caring for each other, to have the security of trust based upon commitment to an ongoing relationship, and to have respect for the individuality of each other—these are essential to intimacy. Thus intimacy is not to be defined simply in sexual terms or in just being together all of the time. Intimacy respects a mate's needs for privacy and celebrates the couples need for togetherness. It is a true expression of real freedom between persons of equal worth. Each person remains a distinct self yet the two together become a dynamic unity of being.

The biblical teachings concerning the Trinity offer a powerful analogy to this kind of relationship. In John 17:11, 22–23, Jesus spoke of the oneness which exists in his relationship to the Father even though he speaks to God as Father and describes himself as Son: "Holy Father, keep them in thy name, which thou has given me, that they may be one, even as we are one" (17:11).

Jesus also prayed that his followers would become one with each other as well as one with himself and the Father. Such a oneness is obviously a dynamic unity in which personal identity is retained, yet equality in being exists since it is similar to the unity-in-relationship of the Trinity.

In some manuscripts of Matthew 19:5–6, the same word for *oneness* used in John 17:11 is used to describe the oneness of marriage. Thus the one-flesh union suggests an emotional complementarity in which personal identity is not lost but a complementary relationship is created.

In the writings of the apostle Paul there is also an emphasis on equality and unity in the Trinity. Paul described God as "the head of Christ" (1 Cor. 11:3), yet he also spoke of the eternal equality of Christ and the Father (Phil. 2:6). Once again we sense the differentiation of persons but equality of being. Paul seemed to use the concept of subordination in a manner that is basically functional. Jesus as equal with the Father voluntarily yielded himself for the task of redeeming human life from sin, but he never lost his oneness with the Father. With all of its mystery, the doctrine of the Trinity witnesses to a concept of personal equality between Father, Son, and Holy Spirit, with the only differentiation of personhood being related to the functional tasks of each person in the Godhead.

In the one-flesh union of marriage, by analogy, the oneness which is possible is a dynamic unity of persons in which equality of personhood exists yet functional subordination to one another also exists for the fulfillment of tasks related to family life.

Bearing Equal Responsibility for Sin

Another facet of human personhood which is clear in the Bible is that every person, male or female, bears an equal responsibility for sin. "All have sinned and fall short of the glory of God," said Paul to the Romans (3:23) since "we all once lived in the passions of our flesh, following the desires of body and mind, and so we were by nature children of wrath, like the rest of mankind" (Eph. 2:3). There is no distinction made here between male and female—all are sinners. Let us examine briefly how this fact of sin is established as described in Genesis 3 as well as relevant passages of the New Testament.

We become sinners, first, *by lack of faith in God.* When Eve was approached by the tempter, she was challenged on the issue of her faith commitment to the Word of God. God had said not to touch or eat of the forbidden fruit "lest you die," but the tempter responded, "you will not die" (Gen. 3:3–4). Eve personally chose to disbelieve God and to have faith in the word of the tempter. Ever since that day, men and women have become sinners by refusing to have faith in God's revelation of himself. The experience of the Christ bears eloquent testimony to the human failure to have faith in God and its tendency to rely upon the voices that lead to destruction.

We become sinners, secondly, *by yielding to temptation.* When her faith in God became weak, Eve yielded to the temptation of that which was "good for food," a "delight to the eyes," and would "make one wise" (Gen. 3:6). As is so often true, the temptation to sin is rationalized as something which will benefit us and therefore is worth doing. The belief that the end justifies the means is a popular ethic in virtually all cultures!

If the story had stopped at this point, we might be willing to say that Eve only was the transgressor in this case (see 1 Tim. 2:14). In Genesis 3:6, however, the Bible records that "she also gave some to her husband, and he ate." Adam, to whom the commandment had first been given, joined Eve rather easily in eating the forbidden fruit and thus became responsible for his transgression as well.

In fact, Paul directly attributed the entry of sin into the world to the sin of Adam, not of Eve, in Romans 5. Death, the consequence of sin, "reigned from Adam to Moses, even over those whose sins were not like the transgression of Adam, who was a type of the one to come" (v. 14). He acknowledged that "the serpent deceived Eve by his cunning" (2 Cor. 11:3), but he included Adam in the act of transgression.

So today both men and women equally become sinners by yielding to the temptations of self-centeredness and rebellion against the way that God has set before us.

We, therefore, are *personally accountable to God's revelation of law and grace.* As Paul emphasized in Romans 3 and in Ephesians 2, all human beings are accountable to God for sin and salvation. The Jews, the Gentiles—all have failed to be what God desired. All are under judgment for sin.

But just as all are sinners, all are objects of the redeeming grace of God made possible by the death and resurrection of Jesus Christ (Eph. 2:8–10). A man of faith cannot assume accountability for his wife's lack of faith, and a wife cannot bear her husband's accountability for sin. Some men would evidently like for it to be so, as the hymn parody suggests: "Take my wife, and let her be/Consecrated, Lord, to thee!" Each man and each woman must bear personal accountability for sin and offer personal commitment to Christ as Savior and Lord. As Paul affirmed in Romans, "So each of us shall give account of himself to God" (14:12). The persons in Christian marriage are equally responsible for sin and equally invited to faith in Christ.

Achieving Equal Personhood in Jesus Christ

Since men and women are equally sinners and equally invited to become Christians by faith in Christ, it must follow that men and women achieve equal personhood in Jesus Christ. Support for this affirmation can be found in the life and teachings of Jesus as well as in the letters of the apostle Paul. Inasmuchas Paul was highly influential in shaping the understanding of the Christian faith, it is important to examine the implications of his teachings for our understanding of personhood in Christ.

Equality in the Ministry of Jesus

As we read the Gospel accounts of Jesus' ministry and teachings, we discover some startling illustrations of his acceptance of persons on the basis of equality. Actually there is more support for this concept in his actual life experience with people than in his recorded teachings.

Jesus made no distinction between male and female in his ministry to their needs. He responded as readily to the particular needs of the woman at the well in Samaria (John 4:7–42) as he did to needs of Zacchaeus, the tax collector, in Jericho (Luke 19:2–10). He offered his forgiveness as freely to the woman caught in the act of adultery (John 8:1–11) as he did to the paralytic brought to him by four friends (Mark 2:1–12). He cleansed a leprous man (Matt. 8:1–4) and healed the daughter of a woman of faith (Matt. 15:22–28). He stopped the woman's hemorrhage of blood (Matt. 9:20–22) as quickly as he opened the eyes of blind men (Matt. 9:27–30). Female and male alike were restored to wholeness in his love and grace.

Jesus broke the cultural traditions defining male/female roles in public. The two most dramatic illustrations of his refusal to be bound by the dominant cultural norms of his day are recorded in John 4:4–42 and John 12:2–3.

The first reference is to the experience of Jesus with the woman at the well in Samaria. In the biblical account, Jesus came to the well while journeying and asked a woman to give him a drink of water. This sounds so simple to our modern ears but in Jesus' day the implications were tremendous. Jewett points to the strangeness of the event when he remarks that "this woman was not only a *woman,* not only a *sinful* woman, but a sinful *Samaritan* woman!"[11] Jewish custom forbade speaking to a woman in public when unacquainted and definitely forbade any public contact between Jews and half-breed Samaritans. Yet Jesus was not bound by the customs of his neighbors. He broke through their restrictiveness to accept this sinful Samaritan woman as a person of worth and in so doing gave her a new identity as a person.

In John 12:2–3 Jesus is in the home of Mary and Martha. During the course of the evening meal, Mary broke open a container of scented ointment to anoint the feet of Jesus. She then wiped his feet with her long hair. Once again we must remember the customs of the day in order to understand the significance of this event. In the first place, an unmarried woman was forbidden to touch the body of a male. Secondly, to let down her hair in public was a highly immodest act. But when she was rebuked by the men present at the supper, Jesus honored her tribute to him as fitting and acceptable.

These are but two examples of Jesus' refusal to allow cultural barriers to reduce women from persons to objects. If we follow his example as well as his teachings, we can never allow the cultural expectations of the New Testament world to blind us to the fundamental personhood of both male and female.

Jesus invited both women and men to follow him. The invitation to discipleship came to men and women. In *The New*

English Bible translation of Matthew 16:24–26, the translators have captured well the idea of the new personhood in Christ that comes through discipleship. Jesus said, "If anyone wishes to be a follower of mine, he must leave self behind; he must take up his cross and come with me. Whoever cares for his own safety is lost; but if a man will let himself be lost for my sake, he will find his true self." "Man" in this passage refers to human beings or persons not males as distinct from females.

We are well aware of the many men who responded to this call to discipleship and new selfhood. Sometimes we forget that women also heard it and responded. Matthew tells us that many women were at the cross "who had followed Jesus from Galilee, ministering to him" (27:55).

The authors of *All We're Meant to Be* provide a fitting summary to this brief treatment of Jesus' attitude toward women and culture. "He treated women not primarily as females but as human beings. Without sentimentality, condescension, or undemanding indulgence, he accepted them as persons in a way that moved them to repentance and love."[12]

Equality in the Teachings of Paul

Many of the interpreters who agree that Jesus exemplified an attitude of acceptance of women which honored their personhood believe that Paul is the culprit in making women second-class citizens of the kingdom. In our brief treatment of his teachings we will not be able to wrestle with all of the arguments that his letters have caused, but we will present a perspective in which to study Paul's statements concerning women.

Paul's interpretation of the gospel declares the equality of men and women in redemption. There is only one gospel for all—the message of salvation by grace through faith in Jesus Christ as Savior and Lord. While writing to the Corinthians, Paul declared, "For I decided to know nothing among you except Jesus Christ and him crucified" (1 Cor. 2:2). He rebuked the Galatians for "turning to a different gospel" but quickly added, "not that there is another gospel" (1:6–7). The one gospel is directed toward women in the same way that it is toward men. This is why Paul in Philippi could go out to the place of prayer by the riverside to sit down and speak about Jesus to the women gathered there (Acts 16:13). It was in response to this message by Paul that Lydia, the first convert in Europe, was converted and baptized (16:14–15).

Romans 5 contains one of Paul's most powerful discussions of the full impact of the gospel. In it he pointed out that Christ's death demonstrates the love of God for human beings who rejected God's will and became enemies of grace. Through the acceptance of that love, hostility was overcome by reconciliation and a new life was begun. All of this happened to overcome the sin problem initiated by "one man's trespass." In Christ, "one man's act of righteousness leads to acquittal and life for all men" (Rom. 5:18). As we read the passage, we must understand that the Greek term translated "man" or "men" is the word for human being or individual, not the word for male. "All men" is like the "Adam" of Genesis 5:2 which is translated man.

Similarly, both men and women become God's "workmanship, created in Christ Jesus for good works, which God prepared before-hand, that we should walk in them" (Eph. 2:10). Salvation by grace through faith is the one and only way to fulfill God's righteousness—for male and female.

The most precise statement of this equality, however, is recorded in Paul's letter to the Galatians. In his argument for the authenticity of the gospel as a fulfillment of God's revelation through the law given to Israel, Paul declared that "in Christ you are all sons of God, through faith" (3:26); that is, all have the status which sons enjoy as inheritors of the father's estate. Because in their baptism they "have put on Christ" as the essence of personhood, "there is neither Jew nor Greek, there is neither slave nor free, there is neither male nor female;

for you are all one in Christ Jesus" (3:27–28). The phrase dealing with male and female literally reads, "there is not male and female."

Certainly Paul was not arguing for the obliteration or denial of the evident differences in male and female as physical/emotional/spiritual persons. In other passages he explicitly encouraged the proper recognition of such differences. But Paul did affirm without qualification the fact that male and female come equally to Christ and equally put on Christ in their affirmation of faith and subsequent baptism. As female and male they can say with Paul, "I have been crucified with Christ; it is no longer I who live, but Christ who lives in me; and the life I now live in the flesh I live by faith in the Son of God, who loved me and gave himself for me" (Gal. 2:20). There can be no clearer affirmation of the equal worth of male/female as persons than this.

Paul's letters commend the contributions of men and women to the work of Christ through the churches. As one reads the epistles Paul wrote to the various churches, there is ample evidence of the significant service given by women to the ministry of the churches.

Lydia, converted at the riverside in Philippi, opened her home as a place to begin a young church (Acts 16:15). Priscilla and her husband Aquila were companions of Paul in his secular work as well as the work of the gospel (Acts 18:1–4; Rom. 16:3–4). In addition they instructed Apollos, the Alexandrian convert who preached so mightily from the Scriptures, in the fuller understanding of the gospel (Acts 18:24–26).

Phoebe, a deaconess of the church at Cenchreae, is commended by Paul as one who has been "a helper of many and of myself as well" (Rom. 16:1–2). The word translated "helper" suggests not only one who has helped others with her resources but also one who has a place of authority over other people.

Paul also saluted Tryphaena and Tryphosa, two women in the church, and Persis as workers in the Lord (Rom. 16:12).

This word has the interesting meaning of laboring with wearisome effort as teachers in promoting and declaring the gospel. Evidently, men and women shared equally in this task. This fact is also suggested by Paul's word concerning Euodia and Syntyche who "worked hard with me to spread the gospel" (Phil. 4:3, TEV).

Paul's concern for the church's reputation dominated his counsel to women in the young congregations. The passages of Paul's letters which we have considered thus far have emphasized the equality of personhood between men and women in the gospel. However, in his epistles there are several passages which convey an entirely different message about women. These passages are all directed toward the relationship of woman to the church and the family. Since we will be examining the family situation later, let us now consider Paul's responses to women in the church. How do his instructions to women square with the equality of persons emphasized in conversion and new life?

First of all, the fundamental freedom of the gospel must be acknowledged. In 2 Corinthians 3, Paul contrasted life under law in the old covenant and life in the Spirit in the new covenant. He maintained that he was a minister "of a new covenant, not in a written code but in the Spirit; for a written code kills, but the Spirit gives life" (3:6). Furthermore, "the Lord is the Spirit, and where the Spirit of the Lord is, there is freedom" (3:17). This freedom delivers one from depending on codes of behavior as the means of salvation. It is the freedom promised by Jesus when he told the Jews, "You will know the truth, and the truth will make you free . . . . If the Son makes you free, you will be free indeed" (John 8:32,36).

The Galatian letter is often described as Paul's gospel of freedom because in it he attacked the legalism of Judaism and proclaimed the true freedom found in Christ. He declared "for freedom Christ has set us free; stand fast therefore, and do not submit again to a yoke of slavery" (5:1). The life of freedom is life in the Holy Spirit. But how does that freedom come to us? It comes as the free gift of God the Father to men and women who become his children by faith. Christ came to "redeem those who were under the law, so that we might receive adoption as sons. And because you are sons, God has sent the Spirit of his Son into our hearts, crying 'Abba! Father!' " (Gal. 4:5–6). James Stewart, noted Scottish theologian, reminds us that "the keynote of the life of adoption is freedom."[13] As children of God, we live life in relationship to our Father's will made known to us by the Holy Spirit.

Secondly, freedom is to be exercised responsibly. It has always been easy to think of freedom in the gospel as some kind of anarchy in society. If I am free, then I can do whatever I please! But this violently contradicts Paul's understanding of responsible freedom in which the motivation for behavior is the effect of choice on other people.

To the Galatians he said, "You were called to freedom, brethren; only do not use your freedom as an opportunity for the flesh, but through love be servants of one another" (5:13).

To the Corinthians he declared, " 'All things are lawful,' but not all things are helpful. 'All things are lawful,' but not all things build up. Let no one seek his own good, but the good of his neighbor" (1 Cor. 10:23–24). He was free to do all things as long as all was done to the glory of God and as a witness to an unbelieving world (10:31–33). Responsibility for the consequences of practicing one's freedom in social life must always be considered in determining appropriate behavior. Only in this way can one demonstrate that he is a bondservant of the Lord Jesus Christ (1 Cor. 6:12–14) and a child of the Father (Rom. 8:12–17). This basic principle is fundamental to Paul's instructions concerning church worship and service for men and women. At this point, however, we are more concerned with the passages relating to women and their responsible freedom.

Thus our third principle is that women in worship and service must not flaunt or misuse their freedom. The public reputation of the young churches was at stake; Paul would not countenance behavior at worship which would cause the church to suffer a bad reputation. This was not a denial of freedom but an affirmation of responsible freedom.

The three passages which create the most difficulty for interpreters of male/female equality are 1 Corinthians 11:2–16; 14:34–36; and 1 Timothy 2:11–15. Each of these passages deals with some problem concerning women and the church. The first one is concerned with proper dress for women at worship, the second with proper decorum during worship, and the third with women's freedom to teach men.

Most biblical interpreters discuss the Corinthian passages from the perspective of a church dominated by enthusiasts— a group within a church who claimed to be Spirit led and thus free to do as they pleased in private life and in worship. Gunther Bornkamm in his book *Paul* points out that Paul consistently rebuked those who allowed their freedom to cause problems in the body and in the community (5:1 ff. and 6:1 ff.). Instead Paul emphasized that life in the Spirit is responsible for the effect of its behavior on others.

Women converts in Corinth may have been particularly eager to demonstrate their newfound freedom in Christ by abandoning the social roles of dress expected in worship. In 1 Corinthians 11:2–16 there is a long discussion of this problem, and the passage is one of the most difficult in the letter to interpret. Without going into a detailed discussion of the entire passage, we can see in it a rebuke to women who were praying and prophesying in the congregation without wearing veils. According to common usage, the word translated "prophesies" (v. 5) meant to teach, refute, reprove, or speak out in praise of God—all under the divine inspiration of God's Spirit. Paul was not concerned about their prophesying, but he was concerned about the negative influence of doing it unveiled. Scanzoni and Hardesty are certainly right in suggesting that "Paul did not want Christian women to act in such a manner that people would confuse them with either the pagan orgiastic cults where women loosed their hair in ecstatic frenzy, or the gnostics who degraded the body and marriage."[14] Since the veil was symbolic of marriage, to set it aside could be interpreted as rejecting marriage.

The basic principle set forth in the passage is that of responsible freedom: "So, whether you eat or drink, or whatever you do, do all to the glory of God. Give no offense to Jews or Greeks or to the church of God" (1 Cor. 10:31–32).

The second passage (1 Cor. 14:33–36) is found within a chapter discussing Paul's concern for order in worship, especially with regard to the problem of glossolalia or speaking in ecstatic language which was not understood by other people in the worship experience. The enthusiasts, as Bornkamm called them, evidently believed that ecstatic speech was more spiritual than prophecy or preaching which others could understand. Without denying a legitimate place for glossolalia in their private spiritual life, the apostle emphasized the greater importance of preaching in order that all the worshipers might learn from it. "All things should be done decently and in order" (1 Cor. 14:40) was his basic principle in this chapter.

Within that context is found the direct word that "women should keep silence in the churches" (14:34). Whether the women were being rebuked for overzealous and emotional behavior we do not know. In chapter 11 Paul had not forbidden praying or prophesying so it seems possible that his strong reaction is in some way related to the problem of speaking in tongues. Some interpreters believe that these verses were not written by Paul but were inserted later by some unknown scribe who was opposed to the freedom women were expressing in worship. Others interpret this as Paul's demand that women not engage in idle talking or unnecessary chatter during worship. Whatever may have been the original cause for Paul's response, the basic principle remains true. Any behavior which would detract from the church's primary mission was to be stopped. This is not to be taken as a universal command to all believers but a rebuke to the women of Corinth for unseemly behavior.

The third passage is found in 1 Timothy 2:11-15. In this setting, women are commanded to learn in quietness and in submission just as all the believers are to "lead a quiet and peaceable life" (2:2). The same word is used for "quiet" in both verses. It has the meaning of refraining from busyness rather than simply refraining from all speech. Women were also not to "teach or to have authority over men" (2:12). The word for "authority" means to domineer over someone to the point of destroying his selfhood.

It is possible that this drastic word was spoken because of the harmful consequences being caused by the women described in chapter 5 of the letter (vv. 11-15). These women were going from house to house and were apparently teaching false ideas as well as gossiping. Such women certainly would raise Paul's anger in the same way that the Judaizers did in Galatians. To quiet them was essential. If this is the occasion for the command, we see once again a local need that required action rather than a universal law. This instruction was essential in Ephesus in order that the men and women alike would "lead a quiet and peaceable life, godly and respectful in every way" (2:2).

In *The Interpreter's Bible,* Fred D. Gealy has a helpful summary with regard to these New Testament instructions to women in the early church. He says:

Since Christian women had been granted unusual freedom, it was necessary that they should be unusually careful not to become insubordinate or neglectful at home. Otherwise their actions would scandalize and alienate pagans. To upset the order of the family would be to precipitate social revolution and bring ruin on the church.[15]

Paul's writings must always be read against this backdrop of concern for the reputation of the church and its witness to lost people. To be respectful of others "is good, and it is acceptable in the sight of God our Savior, who desires all men to be saved and to come to the knowledge of the truth" (1 Tim. 2:3–4).

Notes

1. Paul K. Jewett, *Man as Male and Female* (Grand Rapids: Wm. B. Eerdman Publishing Co., 1975), p. 24.

2. John Money and Patricia Tucker, *Sexual Signatures: On Being a Man or a Woman* (Boston: Little, Brown and Co., 1975), p. 6.

3. Ibid., p. 5.

4. Ibid., p. 10.

5. Anthony Kosnik, et al, *Human Sexuality: New Directions in American Catholic Thought* (New York: Paulist Press, 1977), p. 82.

6. Jewett, p. 24.

7. George A. F. Knight, *A Christian Theology of the Old Testament* (Richmond: John Knox Press, 1959), pp. 122–123.

8. From *The Bible in Today's English Version*. Old Testament: Copyright © American Bible Society 1976. New Testament: Copyright © American Bible Society 1966, 1971, 1976. Used by permission. Subsequent quotations are marked (TEV).

9. Henry Van Dyke, "A Mile with Me," *Collected Poems*.

10. Clinebell, *The Intimate Marriage*, chapter 2.

11. Jewett, p. 101.

12. Letha Scanzoni and Nancy Hardesty, *All We're Meant to Be: A Biblical Approach to Women's Liberation* (Waco: Word Books, 1975), p. 56.

13. James S. Stewart, *A Man In Christ* (New York: Harper and Bros., no date), p. 254.

14. Scanzoni and Hardesty, p. 65.

15. Fred D. Gealy, "First Timothy, Exegesis," *The Interpreter's Bible*, Vol. XI, George Buttrick, ed. (New York: Abingdon, 1955), p. 535.

III

Equality and Submission in Life

In the preceding chapter primary attention was given to the emphasis on equality in the teachings of Jesus and Paul with some attention to related Old and New Testament passages. I have said that male and female are equal persons in their creation in the image of God, that they are equally sinners through personal trangression of God's will, and that they are equally invited to forgiveness and salvation by grace through faith in Jesus Christ. As redeemed persons, male and female are equally accountable for using their newfound freedom responsibly.

Now we must examine the relationship of this equality to the New Testament emphasis on submission as one of the expected demonstrations of Christian faith in human relationships. Are equality and submission complementary concepts, or are they in serious opposition to each other? To deal with this question is the challenge of this chapter.

The Meaning of Submission

Most of the New Testament references to submission use the Greek word *hupotasso* which can be translated as "subjecting oneself or being subjected or being subordinate to a person or persons in authority." The term originally had a military usage in defining the authority levels between ranks and in some of the New Testament usages this idea is quite prominent. For example, in his discussion of the Christians's relationship to the state, Paul declared, "Let every person be subject to the governing authorities" (Rom. 13:1) because of the fear of punishment as well as because of Christian conscience. In this usage of *hupotasso,* obedience to authority is required by the state's ability to enforce such obedience. Any lack of obedience or submission would be punished, therefore involuntary obedience could be demanded by the state. For the Christian, however, some degree of voluntary response was also to be given because of the desire to honor God by obedience to authority in the secular life. The same term is used in Titus 3:1: "Remind them to be submissive to rulers and authorities, to be obedient," and a related word with similar meaning is found in Peter's instruction, "Be subject for the Lord's sake to every human institution" (1 Pet. 2:13).

In the Christian's relationship to secular power, there is a basic inequality of power and status between the state and the individual believer, even in a democratic form of government. This definite hierarchy of authority is reflected in the New Testament command to submit to or be subordinate to the higher powers.

Christians in the first century were well acquainted with this kind of authority. Many were slaves whose unchristian masters treated them harshly yet whose authority they had to obey. Husbands had legal authority over their wives and often expressed that authority in dictatorial ways. The power of rulers in various levels of government was often used to defraud and destroy people in the society.

In other situations, however, the New Testament commanded obedience because the persons possessing authority were worthy of respect. Paul, in Romans 13:4, assumed the integrity of governing persons which makes them worthy of being respected. In 1 Peter 2:18, some slave owners were identified as "kind and gentle" even though others were "overbearing." Christians were expected to be submissive in either situation, but there would obviously be a difference in personal response to authority which was worthy of respect in contrast to that which was harsh and cruel.

This kind of subordination was to be given to parents (Luke 2:51), masters of slaves (Titus 2:9; 1 Pet. 2:18), church officials (1 Pet. 5:5), and to secular authorities as discussed above. In addition, it was expected in the wife-husband relationship as well as in the believer's relationship to God (1 Cor. 15:28; Heb. 12:9; Jas. 4:7) and to Christ (Eph. 5:24).

There is another meaning given to *hupotasso* which introduces a distinctly Christian element into the concept of submission. In one of the widely accepted lexicons of the Greek-English languages, *hupotasso* is defined as "submission in the sense of voluntary yielding in love"[1] with specific reference to its usage in the letters of Paul and Peter. Submission is the yieldedness given by one person to another on the basis of voluntary choice because of loving relationships. Paul encouraged this kind of self-giving in his command for mutual submission in Ephesians 5:21. He also encouraged it in his instruction to the Corinthian church to be submissive in love to the family of Stephanas and other workers for Christ in their midst (1 Cor. 16:16). The apostle Peter described such submissiveness when he said, "Likewise you that are younger be subject to the elders. Clothe yourselves, all of you, with humility toward one another" (1 Pet. 5:5).

In the military use of the term "to be subject to," submission to authority is expected and can be commanded with the threat of punishment if obedience is not given. In the intimate relationship of the church and the family, however, submission as yieldedness in love is a voluntary act of the believer.

The Theology of Voluntary Submission

Voluntary submissiveness in Christian experience is grounded in the voluntary yieldedness in love demonstrated by Jesus Christ. According to Luke's Gospel, Jesus' submission was first expressed in his own family, "He went down with them and came to Nazareth, and was obedient to them" (Luke

2:51). His submission was demonstrated also at his baptism (Matt. 3:13–17). The submission of Jesus was critically tested in Gethsemane (Matt. 26:36–44) when submission to God's will meant acceptance of the cross. His submission was completed at Calvary where he cried out, "Father, into thy hands I commit my spirit!" (Luke 23:46).

Paul interpreted this submission of Jesus to the Father as the means by which salvation is offered to sinful humanity (Rom. 5:6–11) and as the prelude to his lordship over all of life (1 Cor. 15:24–28; Phil. 2:5–11). But the submission is not that of an inferior to a superior: It is the yieldedness in love of a son to the Father (John 17:20–23; Col. 1:13–20), the self-giving of equality.

I like John Taylor's description of Jesus' relationship to the Father:

God was the never-forgotten presence, yet Jesus' relation to God was never dutiful; it was ardent and glad and totally relaxed. It expressed the absolute acceptance of his creaturehood and an untroubled dependence, without a shadow of subservience.[2]

In the Chrisitian life, voluntary submission to one another in love is one way of letting the mind of Christ be revealed in human relationships (Phil. 2:5). To have the mind of Christ in our intimate relationships with each other may also involve dependence without subservicnce when love makes us equals.

Voluntary yieldedness in love is required in the believer's acceptance of salvation. The New Testament clearly describes the offer of salvation as a gift of grace to which persons must respond in a decision of faith and acceptance (Eph. 2:8–10; Rom. 5:15–17). There is no way to experience the new life in Christ without yielding one's personal sovereignty to the lordship of Christ. Jesus described discipleship in terms of the surrendered self (Matt. 16:24–27) by which one discovers the true meaning of life. Paul emphasized personal responsibility for accepting Christ's lordship (Rom. 14:7–12) and concluded that "each of us will have to answer for himself" (14:12, NEB). In Galatians, Paul summed up beautifully the relationship between surrender, love, and salvation when he said: "Our hope of attaining that righteousness which we eagerly await is the work of the Spirit through faith. If we are in union with Christ Jesus circumcision makes no difference at all, nor does the want of it; the only thing that counts is faith active in love" (5:5–6, NEB). The only way to salvation is to voluntarily accept by faith the offer of redemption made possible by the cross and the empty tomb and which is actualized in one's heart by the Holy Spirit's response to faith (Gal. 6:7–9).

Voluntary yieldedness in love is necessary in most Christian traditions if the believer is to become a participating member of a local church. When an individual unites with a local body of believers, that person is implicitly yielding a part of self to the community of faith. There is expectation from the church that the believer will attend worship, engage in study for Christian growth, give a regular offering to help the church carry on its ministry, and become involved to some degree in the fellowship of mutual supportiveness of the membership.

This necessity for personal yieldedness to the body is most clearly expressed in a congregational polity in which the members of the church publicly vote on the acceptance of new members. The individual seeking to unite with the fellowship must be willing to yield a portion of personal sovereignty in the decision to enter into covenant with the body of believers who then choose to accept him or her.

In addition, the church member is expected to give honor and obedience to the leaders of the church. The writer of the epistle to the Hebrews was most explicit about this. He instructed his readers, first of all, to "remember your leaders, those who first spoke God's message to you; and reflecting upon the outcome of their life and work, follow the example of their faith" (13:7, NEB). Then he declared that Christians should "obey your leaders and submit to them" (13:7). In this instruc-

tion we do not have an expectation of unqualified obedience
to the ministers of the church, of course, but the Christian is
expected to respect those chosen to serve in the vocational
leadership of the church.

*Voluntary submissiveness is also to be expressed in the believ-
er's relationship to the institutions of society in which he lives.*
Paul expected Christian obedience to secular authorities (Rom.
13:1–6; Titus 3:1), submission of slaves to their masters (Eph.
6:5–8; Titus 2:9–10), and faithfulness in paying taxes (Rom.
13:7). This yieldedness to society is for the purpose of exalting
the lordship of Christ in the Christian witness to the community. In Taylor's words, "To say 'Jesus is Lord' pledges us to
find the effects of his cross and resurrection in the world, not
just in our inner lives, nor in the church."[3] Our mission is to
live the ordinary life of people in the world but in a conscious-
ness that we are called upon to be salt and light to that world.
The quality of our life is to be a testimony to the Lord of
life.

Of all the social institutions in which a vital Christian witness
is needed, the family is most important for the formation of
Christian character. First Corinthians, Ephesians, Colossians,
and 1 Peter give explicit attention to this need for yieldedness
in love in family relationships, but an essential focus is on
mutual yielding to one another as an expression of one's Christian faith.

The Application of Mutual Submission

Many of the books describing male/female relationships for
Christians place great stress upon the need of the wife to be
submissive to her husband. In the light of our discussion thus
far, there is ample evidence that the submission which we
have called "voluntary yieldedness in love" is essential to all
relationships in the family just as it is in other social relationships of Christians. Such submission is therefore a *mutually
reciprocal* relationship.

To emphasize submission for the wife and ignore it for the husband is to do an injustice to Paul's instructions in Ephesians 5:21. Many New Testament interpreters agree with Lehaman Strauss when he points out that "submission in the home is not something enjoined upon the woman only; it is a mutual relationship.[4]

An Overview of Ephesians

Since this theme of mutual submission is explicity set forth in Ephesians, let us now examine Paul's letter. Because the entire book is important to our discussion, we will begin with a brief overview of it. Particular attention will then be devoted to Ephesians 5:15–21 and 5:22–6:4 in the application of mutual submission to the home.

Paul began the letter with a testimony of praise to God for the blessings he had given in Christ Jesus (1:3–14), then moved quickly into a reminder to the believers of the hope they have because of God's power revealed in the Lord (1:15–23). In chapter 2 Paul set forth what has been called the Magna Charta of salvation by grace through faith (2:1–10) and explains the new human oneness made possible through Christ since the barriers to human relatedness have been broken down by the cross (2:11–22). Paul testified to his own apostleship and concluded with a ringing doxology of praise to the Father and Son (3:1–21).

Chapter 4 makes a transition from the discussion of theological foundations for Christian faith to the practice of Christian living in the appeal for believers to "lead a life worthy of the calling to which you have been called" (v. 1). This "calling" is not the call to vocational Christian ministry but is the call to be a committed Christian which comes to every person accepting Jesus Christ as Savior and Lord. One's whole life-style is to reflect the new life created in Christ Jesus which Paul pointed to in Ephesians 2:8–10. Growth toward maturity is to be guided by those persons in the fellowship who are called to devote their lives to Christian ministry in order that the church as the body of Christ may grow in every way (4:7–16). In 4:17 to 5:21 Paul described some of the implications of this new and maturing life-style in explicit terms.

The apostle warned the Christian against drunkenness induced by alcohol but commanded the believer to be "filled with the Spirit" (5:18). Kenneth Wuest points out that "filled" in the Greek text is a present imperative which can be translated, "Be constantly, moment by moment, being controlled by the Spirit."[5]

The Spirit-filled Life

This is an important clause because it introduces three specific evidences of the Spirit-filled life in the verses that follow (5:19–21). Before looking at these statements, however, it is necessary to explain a difference between Paul's words in this text and the popular charismatic belief which understands being "filled with the Spirit" as a second blessing one receives after being saved and which does not come into the lives of all believers when they are converted. In this passage Paul assumed that all believers are filled with the Spirit of God as a normal part of the experience of salvation.

John Taylor's book *The Go-Between God* is an exciting and beautiful book about the work of the Holy Spirit in the Christian mission. Taylor is General Secretary of the Church Missionary Society in England. In his survey of New Testament teachings concerning the Spirit, Taylor declares that "the new relationship with the Spirit and the new relationship with Jesus are indistinguishable. Life 'in the Spirit' is identical with life 'in Christ.' "[6] Taylor could find no New Testament evidence that being filled with the Spirit or living in the Spirit required a second experience of blessing or a second rite that would give the Spirit to the believer. Believing that this is a correct interpretation of the New Testament, I agree that every believer receives or is filled by the Holy Spirit at the time of conversion.

However, it is also important to recognize that the believer must continually yield his life to the power and guidance of God's Spirit if he is to grow in faith and have power to live the Christian life-style of freedom and responsibility which Paul described. Taylor reminds us that this is not easily done by all believers:

Few are they who, after their first awakening, dare trust the Spirit to carry them by way of the wilderness and the dark night into a widening freedom and availability until this manhood of Christ himself is formed in them; but there are many who will either settle for religion without miracle, or try to live by a regular recurrence of the moment of their conversion.[7]

Most of us have heard testimonies by individuals who can recall the Spirit's impact on their lives at the moment of conversion but seem to have no testimony to the living reality of the Spirit in the daily experience of life. No doubt Paul spoke to these individuals when he said, "Do not grieve the Holy Spirit of God, in whom you were sealed for the day of redemption" (4:30). The word translated "grieve" comes from a root word meaning "to cause distress or pain," thus a Christian's refusal to walk daily in the Spirit's power causes distress to the One who makes God real in our hearts.

To trust one's life to the leadership of the Holy Spirit means that we must be willing to listen and free to respond to the new directions that God may give us in our daily life in this world. Jesus said that when the Spirit enters the life of the Christian, he comes as Teacher as well as Comforter. "But the Counselor, the Holy Spirit, whom the Father will send in my name, he will teach you all things, and bring to your remembrance all that I have said to you" (John 14:26). This was the source of Paul's boldness in dealing with the thorny, ethical questions sent to him by the church at Corinth. Since he had no direct word from the Lord on those issues, he gave his own interpretation of the correct way to deal with the problem in the conviction "that is my opinion, and I believe that I too have the Spirit of God" (1 Cor. 7:40, NEB).

As believers who also have the Spirit of God in our lives, we must try to determine what God's will is for our lives in the contemporary world. Taylor again helps us understand this challenge of living in the Spirit when he declares that this kind of life "must have in view not a rule of life but a style of life, an authentic personhood which is consistent because it is under God, and free because it is under the forgiveness of God."[8] Especially as we discuss family relationships, this freedom to be responsive to God's Spirit in our lives must not be fenced in by rules and prohibitions which can thwart Christian growth into authentic personhood. We must not "grieve the Holy Spirit of God" by failing to yield our lives to his guidance because of the dogmatic advice given to us by those who may not understand what God is doing with us in our own experience.

As Paul described the implications of this experience with God's Spirit, he declared that the Spirit-filled life should be one of joy, thankfulness, and mutual submission (5:19–21). To be somewhat technical for a moment, the Greek text has the imperative, "be filled with the Spirit," as a main clause with verses 19–21 as participial clauses modifying the main verb. It can be translated like this:

Be filled with the Spirit (5:18):
Addressing one another in psalms and hymns and spiritual songs, singing and making melody to the Lord with all your heart (5:19);
Giving thanks always and for everything in the name of our Lord Jesus Christ to God the Father (5:20);
Being submissive or subordinate to one another out of reverence for Christ (5:21).

Paul affirmed that these qualities of joy, thankfulness, and mutual submission are distinguishing characteristics of life in the Holy Spirit.

He then applied the meaning of mutual submission to two basic social institutions in which the believers lived—the family and slavery (5:22 to 6:9). Ray Summers makes this point in his commentary on Ephesians:

Paul closes the discussion by saying that in all this we are (to) subject ourselves one to the other in reverence for Christ. This looks backward to all that he has said about the application of redemption in the personal life of the believer. We live our lives in a social framework in relationship one to the other, and that involves the idea of mutual submission one to the other as we walk in love, in light, and in wisdom. This mutual subjection one to the other is carried out in the spirit of reverence which Christ produces within.[9]

The epistle closes with the admonition to put on the armor which God provides in fighting against evil. The believer's strength is in God's Spirit empowering him for the battle to fulfill God's will in the world (6:10–20). The last four verses are closing prayers for the people in Ephesus (6:21–24).

Having briefly surveyed the Ephesian letter, let us now return to where Paul indicated that we are to "be subject to one another out of reverence for Christ" (5:21).

Mutual Submissiveness in Christian Reverence

The instructions Paul gave for social relationships in Ephesians 5:21 to 6:9 are called "a table of household duties" by New Testament interpreters. Similar instructions are included in Colossians 3:18 to 4:1 and 1 Peter 2:13 to 3:7, but it is in Ephesians that mutual subordination is explicitly set forth as the basis for these duties. In each of the passages, however, the basic motivation for obedience to these instructions is the Christian's response to Christ.

Peter said, "Be subject for the Lord's sake to every human institution" (1 Pet. 2:13). In the Colossian letter, Paul introduced the table of household duties by affirming, "whatever you do, in word or deed, do everything in the name of the Lord Jesus" (3:17). But Paul's word in Ephesians is even stronger than either of these. Christians are to subordinate themselves to one another "in the fear of God" (5:21).[10] The Greek word *phobos* is translated "reverence" in the Revised Standard Version, *Today's English Version* and the *New English Bible*. In *The Living Bible, Paraphrased* it is translated as "honor."[11]

Reverence, honor, and respect are appropriate elements of *phobos*, but they may not capture the essential truth that mutual subordination is directly related to the acceptance of Christ as Savior and Lord through submission to his will. The original connotation of the term is similar to the Old Testament idea of "the fear of the Lord." Man recognizes his need for God and humbly surrenders himself to his Creator. Thus Paul chose a word which sharpens the claim of discipleship on social relationships in the family of faith.

On the basis of this submission to Christ, believers are to "be subject to one another." Some interpreters insist on the idea of "submission" or "surrender" as the proper meaning of this phrase while others prefer the idea of "subordination." This may seem like an argument over such small differences that it does not have any meaning for you. However, in our English language there is a different connotation given to *submission* than to *subordination*. The dictionary describes *submission* as "surrender of person and power to the control of another" whereas *subordination* is "to place in rank or order of position." The participle "submitting yourselves to one another" (KJV) does demand personal yielding to the claims of relationship but it is not given at the expense of personhood.

Markus Barth, noted son of the famous Karl Barth, has written an excellent and detailed commentary on Ephesians in which he argues for subordination as the appropriate meaning of this verse. His conclusion is that "the participles or imperatives calling for subordination may well contain an appeal to free and responsible agents that can only be heeded voluntarily, but never by the elimination or breaking of the human will, not to speak of servile submissiveness."[12] His position is complementary to our discussion of yieldedness as a voluntary act which respects the personhood of the individuals in the family or church.

The demand for mutuality in self-giving is a dramatically new teaching about social relationships. Women, slaves, and citizens were always expected to be subordinate or submissive to superior persons, but to expect men to accept women on equal terms of self-giving or slave-owners to accept slaves was like a streak of lightning in a blue sky! It is for this reason that verse 21 must be interpreted as a prelude to all that is included in 5:22 to 6:9. Barth insists that "the unique message of Ephesians is silenced whenever the dominant position of v. 21 over the *Haustafel* (table of household duties) and the peculiarly startling content of this verse are neglected.[13]

How, then, is this subordination or yieldedness to be understood since Paul maintained that it is one of the distinguishing marks of the Spirit-filled life?

In his *Ephesians and Colossians in the Greek New Testament,* Kenneth Wuest interprets *hupotasso* in Ephesians 5:21 as "the opposite of self-assertion, the opposite of an independent, autocratic spirit. It is the desire to get along with one another, being satisfied with less than one's due, a sweet reasonableness of attitude.[14] W. Curtis Vaughan of Southwestern Baptist Theological Seminary amplifies this definition when he says that it "denotes that attitude of reciprocal deference that becomes and marks out those who are filled with the Spirit. It is opposed to rudeness, haughtiness, selfish preference for one's own opinions, and stubborn insistence on one's own rights."[15]

If one compares these definitions of submission with Paul's description of love in 1 Corinthians 13:4-7, the similarities are obvious. Therefore we affirm again that submission in Ephesians 5:21 can very appropriately be translated as "voluntary yieldedness in love." Such yieldedness is to be expressed by each family member toward the other—not just by the wife to her husband. It is to this theme that we turn in the next chapter.

Notes

1. William F. Arndt and F. Wilbur Gingrich, *A Greek-English Lexicon of the New Testament and Other Early Christian Literature*, 4th ed. rev., (Cambridge: Cambridge University Press, 1957), p. 855.

2. John V. Taylor, *The Go-Between God* (Philadelphia: Fortress Press, 1973), p. 93.

3. Ibid., p. 135.

4. Lehman Strauss, *Devotional Studies in Galatians and Ephesians* (New York: Loizeaux Bros., 1957), p. 205.

5. Kenneth S. Wuest, *Ephesians and Colossians in the Greek New Testament* (Grand Rapids: Wm. B. Eerdmans Publishing Co., 1953), p. 128.

6. Taylor, p. 110.

7. Ibid., p. 48.

8. Ibid., p. 165.

9. Ray Summers, *Ephesians: Pattern for Christian Living* (Nashville: Broadman Press, 1960), p. 116.

10. From the King James Version of the Bible. Subsequent references are marked (KJV).

11. Copyright © Tyndale House Publishers, Wheaton, Illinois, 1971. Used by permission.

12. Markus Barth, *Ephesians: Introduction, Translation and Commentary on Chapters 4—6* (Garden City, New York: Doubleday and Co., 1974), p. 609.

13. Ibid., p. 610.

14. Wuest, p. 128.

15. W. Curtis Vaughan, *The Letter to the Ephesians* (Nashville: Convention Press, 1963), p. 113.

IV

Mutual Submission in
Family Relationships

In the basic family unit, there are four primary relations: wife to husband, husband to wife, children to parents, and parents to children. In addition, there are the relationships of children to each other and the relationship of the basic family unit to any other family members who might reside in the home. Within the purpose of our discussion, attention will be given to the four primary relationships in a Christian home and to the husband-wife relationship in a marriage that is religiously mixed. The key resource will be Ephesians 5:21 to 6:4 with supplementary materials drawn from other New Testament sources.

Our basic assumption is that in the context of Ephesians, Paul was addressing the Christian family—one in which mutual yieldedness in love is based upon the family's acceptance of Christ as Lord of the home. Therefore all other patterns of relationship are built upon the foundation of faith in Christ. Let us now review the first pattern of relationship which Paul describes—the wife to her husband.

The Wife to Her Husband
(Eph. 5:22–24; Col. 3:18; Titus 2:4–5)

In the Greek and Hebrew cultures existent at the time of the New Testament writings, the man had legal authority over his wife and she had no choice other than to accept that authority. In most cases, as we discussed in the first chapter, these marriages were arranged by negotiations between the parents

of the couple and neither of the marriage partners may have
had much involvement in the choice of their mate. Scanzoni
and Hardesty describe the status of wives in the Greek culture
as "secluded and closely guarded to insure that all offspring
were those of the husband. Regarded as permanent minors,
a woman's person and property were controlled by a guard-
ian—father, husband, husband's heir, or even the state."[1] In
the ancient Hebrew culture, "whether single or married, she
was under the jurisdiction of some male; she was never her
own person. Betrothal terms were the same as those of pur-
chase."[2]

Thus a woman in marriage was required to accept the authority of her husband, but Paul went beyond this in Ephesians.
He set forth a new interpretation of authority and required
from the Christian wife a new attitude toward her Christian
husband. Her relationship to him is to reflect her voluntary
yieldedness in love based upon her own experience of salvation
through yielding her life to Christ.

She is to accept his Christian personhood. Since the basic
assumption of the relationship described in Ephesians is a marriage between Christians, the wife is to affirm her husband
as one who also has become a new person in Christ Jesus.
Even though the marriage may have been arranged for her
by her parents, she adds a new dimension of response to the
relationship. She now accepts him as a Christian husband to
whom she can truly give herself in love and respect.

Contemporary Christian marriages are usually stronger
when the husband is a firm believer in Christ as Savior and
Lord. The new sense of selfhood which Christ promises to those
who follow him enables the man to find greater strength for
his life as a husband and also enables the wife to affirm her
personhood in the home.

She is to respect him in the family as a responsible person.
In Ephesians Paul used the concept of male headship as illustrative of male responsibility in the marriage because this idea

was accepted and universally recognized in the New Testament world. The ancient family was patriarchal; the husband was lord and master of his household. When we translate the idea of headship into our own day, the concept of responsibility seems to me to be a very adequate interpretation. The husband's headship is modeled on the example of Christ's headship in the church which is an authority expressed through love. Authority is not domination but responsible headship in the family.

When the husband exercises this kind of headship, the wife's response is to be one of voluntary yieldedness in love because of her respect for him. She finds him worthy of trust and self-giving and voluntarily gives herself to him as a Christian wife. In doing so she fulfills Paul's instruction, "and let the wife see that she respects her husband" (Eph. 5:33).

She is to love him. Even though in the Ephesians passage Paul did not command the wife to love her husband, he did make this command in the epistle to Titus. In Titus 2:4–5, the older women are encouraged to teach the younger wives "to love their husbands and children." The terms used in this letter can literally be translated as "love with affection."

It may seem strange to our modern generation that Paul did not include the command to love in his instructions to Christian wives in the Ephesian letter. However, we need to remember that Paul may have been addressing one of the more common problems of the day in his insistence that wives respect their husbands. A woman had to live under the authority of her husband because this was established by law, but she could still make his life miserable if she did not respect him as a husband and father. For Paul to insist on respect was to apply one basic quality of authentic love to marriage under an ancient system of life. In our own time, respect still remains as one of the very necessary qualities of love if love is to grow through the years that a couple remain married.

The contemporary Christian wife usually will not need to

be commanded to love her husband since most people in the United States describe their reason for marriage as "being in love." We may not always be clear as to just what that term implies, but love is considered to be the necessary prelude to marriage. In Paul's day love was not a prerequisite even though it might have been present. Respect was more essential in the wife to husband relationship than love, but affectional love was still expected in a Christian marriage as the letter to Titus indicates.

The Husband to His Wife
(Eph. 5:25–31; Col. 3:19; 1 Pet. 3:7)

If Paul's instructions to Christian wives were startling in their demand for a new attitude toward husbands, this word to husbands must have been even more controversial to first-century man! Custom required that a man provide adequately for his wife, but first-century marriage customs did not demand love. Certainly many husbands in the Greek and Hebrew cultures did love their wives, but Paul maintained that *agape* love is essential in the husband to wife relationship.

The verb *agapaō* is the strongest term for love in the New Testament. Its basic meaning is to esteem and value the object of love to such a degree that one gives his best for the love object. God so valued the world that he gave his only Son to redeem it from sin. The Christian husband is to so value his wife that he is willing to voluntarily yield his life into partnership with her to establish a Christian marriage. It is in light of the meaning of love that we affirm the need for the husband to understand the place of submission in his relationship to his wife. It is impossible to love one's wife in accord with this biblical description of love without voluntarily surrendering an autocratic spirit of domination over her life. Instead, a man is to accept his wife as an equal partner in creating a marital relationship which honors that kind of love. The husband's voluntary yieldedness in love fulfills the command to be submissive or subordinate to one another in reverence for Christ.

What, then, are the implications of the New Testament instructions for Christian husbands recorded in the letters of Paul and Peter?

He accepts her Christian personhood. Some years ago a family sociologist suggested that the problem with contemporary American marriage is that it is designed for only one and a half persons! In his evaluation of American culture, he felt that a wife was not generally accepted as a whole person. This is no doubt true in many marriages today, but in the Christian marriage the wife is to be accepted as a person whom Christ has loved into new selfhood. That selfhood is every bit equal to the selfhood of the male. Thus we affirm that the husband's acceptance of and respect for his wife's Christian personhood is fundamental to the biblical teachings on marriage.

He demonstrates sacrificial love (Eph. 5:25–27). The Greek present tense of the imperative "love your wives" indicates that his love is to be a habitual, on-going response to her. He is to make a habit of loving his wife in such a way that she knows she truly is loved. Thus the husband's love must be one of active expression rather than theoretical acceptance if it is to be patterned on the example of Christ's love for the church. Love like this demands the voluntary yieldedness of the man to the woman in love.

Ray Summers refers to the meaning of the verb describing Christ's love for the church as illustrative of the one supreme act of love which Christ accomplished on the cross. "This means," Summers says, "that he loved the church to the extent that he gave up his own best interest out of consideration for the best interest of the Church." This is the example by which a man is to evaluate his love for his wife. "He is to love his wife to the extent that he will give up his own best interest in order that the best interest of his wife shall be advanced."[3] His authority is actually expressed in his self-giving.

This is a very difficult concept for many of us to accept easily!

Perhaps it will help us to realize that Jesus' own disciples had difficulty understanding the new meaning of authority that he taught them.

On one occasion the disciples of Jesus became involved in an argument concerning who would have the place of authority and prominence when the kingdom of God was established in power. In Jesus' response to their controversy, he taught a basic principle of the way in which believers are to demonstrate their closeness to him: "You know that the rulers of the Gentiles lord it over them, and their great men exercise authority over them. It shall not be so among you; but whoever would be great among you must be your servant, and whoever would be first among you must be your slave; even as the Son of man came not to be served but to serve, and to give his life a ransom for many" (Matt. 20:25–28).

In the Christian life, authority is surrendered and self-giving is required. This is also applicable to the husband-wife relationship as expressed by Paul.

Express caring love (Eph. 5:28–30). As Paul reflected on the mutual commitment of marriage, he told the husband that his love for his wife is to be similar to the love he has for his own body. He is to have a caring love for her just as he has a caring love for himself. Paul was not being selfish in this admonition even though it might sound like it. Rather he was trying to give tangible expression to the meaning of the one-flesh union which he emphasized in 5:31. The husband and the wife are one in such a fundamental way that the husband's care for her is giving nurture to a part of his own being.

Another illustration of the close relationship between husband and wife as one flesh is suggested in Paul's discussion of sexual experience in marriage (1 Cor. 7:3–5). He described marriage as a one-to-one relationship of male and female in which their sexual life is to reflect their equality in personhood. The husband, according to Paul, has needs or rights assumed in the marriage contract which the wife is to honor by giving herself to him sexually. This idea was already accepted in the male-dominated society of the New Testament world, but Paul seems to have gone beyond society's expectations in his concern that the wife's needs be satisfied as well. His word is, "the husband should give to his wife her conjugal rights, and likewise the wife to her husband."

Perhaps the most dramatic impact of this discussion is the apostle's insistence that the wife exercises authority over her husband's body in the same way that he has authority over hers. The word translated "rule over" in this passage means "to have full and entire authority over the body, to hold the body subject to one's will" according to the Greek lexicon. Thus in the one-flesh union of marriage, the man and woman are equally responsible for meeting the needs of one another and demonstrating proper respect for the personhood of one another represented by the body.

In sociological terms, we might also call caring the instrumental function of love. In the New Testament world the husband was the producer of income as he worked outside the home while his wife was responsible for home functions as well as child nurture. Paul expected the Christian husband to adequately care for his wife since she is dependent upon him for that support.

In many homes of today, the function of providing income is still essentially the husband's task, but in many others the husband and wife share equally in income producing. In these homes the caring function of love will be differently expressed but it is still an essential part of the husband-wife relationship.

Develop understanding love (1 Pet. 3:7). Translations of this verse reflect different interpretations of the meaning of Peter's instruction to husbands, even though most of them share a common understanding of the intent of the passage. In the King James Version, husbands are encouraged to "dwell with them according to knowledge, giving honour unto the wife, as unto the weaker vessel, and as being heirs together of the grace of life, that your prayers be not hindered." In the Revised Standard Version the instruction is to live "considerately with your wives" while Phillips[4] and *The New English Bible* translators prefer the meaning of "understanding" rather than "knowledge" (KJV) or "considerately."

I prefer using the idea of *understanding* as an adequate translation of the Greek term. Phillips' interpretation of the verse is an appropriate one: "Similarly, you husbands should try to understand the wives you live with, honouring them as physically weaker yet equally heirs with you of the grace of life. If you don't do this, you will find it impossible to pray."

We are well aware that complete understanding of another is probably impossible, but in marriage, growth in understanding is essential to development into a more intimate relationship. Paul Tournier, the Swiss psychiatrist and lay theologian who has helped so many people through his books, points to the close connection between love and understanding in his book, *To Understand Each Other:*

It is quite clear that between love and understanding there is a very close link. It is so close that we never know where the one ends and the other begins, nor which of the two is the cause or the effect. He who loves understands, and he who understands loves. One who feels understood feels loved, and one who feels loved feels sure of being understood.[5]

Tournier has also reminded us that in order for understanding to develop, we must want to understand the other person. So the Christian husband is encouraged to seek that understanding relationship with his wife in which their spiritual unity may be developed fully.

What is meant by calling women "the weaker vessel" (KJV) or the "weaker sex" (RSV)? Some interpreters suggest this as a reference to the weakness of Eve in succumbing to the temptation in the Garden; thus, the weakness is spiritual in nature. However, other uses of the same word in the New Testament give more support to physical weakness as the proper implication of this passage. For example, when the disciples fell asleep in the garden of Gethsemane while Jesus prayed, Jesus said to them, "the spirit indeed is willing, but the flesh is weak" (Matt. 26:41). The word translated "weak" is the same as the one in Peter's letter concerning women. It is therefore appropriate to interpret Peter's words as a warning to the husband against taking advantage of his wife's physical weakness in order to dominate her.

Instead, the husband is to honor his wife as an equal partner in the grace of life. The word translated "honor" has the meaning of bestowing great value or respect on a person. Thus one's wife is to be given highest worth or value in the husband's life because of who she is and because of his joint partnership with her in God's grace. In such a relationship there can be no disgrace in the man yielding himself in love to a woman whose value to him is superior to all other earthly benefits. He can agree with the writer of Proverbs who declared: "She is far more precious than jewels" (31:10).

The Child to the Parent
(Eph. 6:1–3; Col. 3:20; 1 Tim. 5:3–8; Luke 2:51)

In this third pattern of relationship, that of child to parent, submission is once again fundamental to the way in which the child responds to his parents. Even though the parents have legal authority over the minor child and a social authority beyond that, the willingness of the child to submit his life to his parents will determine how effective the family guidance will be.

The child is to demonstrate respect for parental authority and responsibility. The child in the biblical family was expected to respect his parents and to obey them promptly. However, many biblical passages describing the family life of a number of the men of God in the Old Testament reveal that this was not always true in the real world of family living. The consequences of disobedience, as well as the consequences of parental permissiveness, are well documented in the life story of Samuel and his sons.

In our own day we have seen a return to a more responsible kind of discipline after a rather long excursion into the psychological pathways of permissiveness in child rearing. We know that unless the child learns self-control and respect for authority in the home there is the possibility of his never adequately coping with the realities of social living.

Dr. W. Wayne Grant, in his excellent book entitled *Growing Parents Growing Children,* points out that "children feel more secure and protected when their parents set rules and regulations and enforce them consistently." He also points out that some parents are hesitant in the use of discipline because they do not want their child emotionally hurt by the abuses of parental discipline. This may be because "it is difficult for some parents to distinguish between firmness which is necessary and the anger which often accompanies their disciplinary efforts." Dr. Grant concludes, however, that "discipline and self-control are necessary for a person to be a creative, successful adult."[6] Thus respect for parental authority is essential to the emotional well-being of the child in later years. This acceptance of parental position is exemplified in the child's willingness to obey parents as Paul said, "in the Lord." The writer of Hebrews gave us an excellent interpretation of the importance of such guidance in his discussion of God's guidance of his children (Heb. 12:3–11).

Parents are to encourage a developing selfhood which will change the child's relationship to the parent. Strict obedience to parents is usually a requirement during the younger years of the child's life, but absolute obedience is not always the best measure of successful child rearing as the child moves on toward adolescence and young adulthood. Internalizing moral responsibility must be achieved by the growing youth if discipline is to fulfill its intended goal, and inner controls are definitely related to the child's sense of self-identity.

Dr. Grant helps us again when he says,

In order for children to grow into well-adjusted adults, they need to love themselves properly; but at the same time, they need to learn inner control and self-discipline in order to live creatively with others. In other words, they need to develop a healthy self-image.[7]

To expect the young adult to subordinate his own growth by continually remaining in a dependent relationship to his parents can be defeating for his own self-identity as a responsible person. The relationship to parents needs to move from dependency to independence to interdependence in which the parents can be friends rather than controllers.

Children are to care for parents in senior years if necessary (1 Tim. 5:3–8,16). As the population grows older through the increasing longevity of both men and women, the possibility that younger adults may have to care for senior adults is increasing.

In the early church, there was a program designed to provide care for older widows who had no one to be responsible for them. The church, however, was not to be made a scapegoat for care if the widow had children or grandchildren who could provide for her in her old age. In 1 Timothy 5:8 there is the strong statement that "if any one does not provide for his relatives, and especially for his own family, he has disowned the faith and is worse than an unbeliever." Christian women were specifically commanded to care for relatives who were widows rather than expect the church to do so (5:16).

Even though senior parents have a primary responsibility to plan for their own future needs, there are times when children must assume a financial responsibility for their care. This does not mean that it is always best for parents to be cared for in the home of the younger adults, but it does place a responsibility on them for helping to determine what care is best and to share in providing it.

The Parent to the Child
(Eph. 6:4; Col. 3:21)

The next pattern of family relationship described by Paul is that of parent to child. Once again we are suggesting that the fulfillment of this parental responsibility is an illustration of mutual submission in the family since parents cannot give this kind of guidance without voluntarily yielding part of their lives to the child in their care for him. In the Ephesians and Colossians passages, Paul spoke directly to fathers. In 1 Timothy, however, the wife is described as having a definite part in child guidance (5:10,14). What is the parental responsibility to children?

Avoid building up resentment. The first word of instruction is "do not provoke your children to anger" (Eph. 6:4) or do not "goad your children to resentment" as *The New English Bible* translates it. Parents are undoubtedly going to make their children mad or angry at times in the practice of discipline. This is to be expected and accepted as normal if the anger does not build up into resentment which can destroy the healthy parent-child relationship.

Such resentment may be caused by parents who are overly strict in their disciplinary methods. They usually have rather perfectionistic ideals for their children and seek to actualize those ideals by harsh punishment when the child's behavior does not please them. Dr. Grant points out that a child reared in this manner "often tends to be a conformist—cooperative, quiet, passive, and self-controlled." However, this outer appearance of acceptance of parental authority may mask the hostility which is buried within the child's emotions. "The time often comes," continues Grant, "when such a child rebels with vengeance against the rigidity and strictness of the home."[8]

The daughter of a Sunday School director in one Southern

Baptist church experienced just such a rebellion. Her father was a very rigid type of person with high expectations that the public behavior of his children would not embarrass the family. The teenage daughter wanted to dress in blue jeans like the other kids in school, but the father was very much opposed to her doing so since blue jeans were not feminine. Tension between father and daughter increased over a two-year period during which time she became more belligerent about her clothes, and he withdrew from any physical touching of love and concern in his relationship with her. Finally she decided to run away from home and began hitchhiking down the highway. The man who picked her up tried to attack her and then left her for dead by the roadside. When taken to a local hospital she required over two hundred stitches in her scalp to repair the damage. Her rebellion had almost cost her life.

The father in this situation had been very concerned that his children do the right thing in public behavior. But in his rigid insistence on strong disciplinary methods, he almost lost his daughter. As he reflected on the experience, he and his wife both recognized that they had really provoked the daughter to resentment. The near tragedy opened up the possibility of finding new ways to relate as a family even when behavior was less than acceptable to the parents.

Practicing the art of loving in the context of Christian grace can help keep parents from provoking resentment in the hearts of their children.

Provide guidance in Christian character formation. The second challenge given to the home is to guide children in the formation of a Christian value system which will enable them to make appropriate moral judgments during their growth process. Paul described this task as bringing them up in "the discipline and instruction of the Lord." The word translated "discipline" describes the education or nurture of children and is not to be understood simply as punishment although punishment is a legitimate aspect of discipline. For example, the same word is used in 2 Timothy where the writer reminded Timothy that Scripture is profitable for "training in righteousness" (3:16). Thus the father is instructed to give his children guidance which will aid their character development.

This guidance is given in *implicit* teaching as well as *explicit* teaching. For instance, parents serve as models for their children in the actual ways that they live out their own moral norms in the home. Their behavior becomes, therefore, an implicit means of teaching through example. Carl Elder provides an excellent resource for evaluating the ways by which children learn moral values in *Values and Moral Development in Children*. He affirms the implicit teaching of moral values when he says, "It is within the family unit that a child comes to be fully human. Moral values are taught and caught through the child's everyday home experiences."[9] If the child, for example, sees his parents go out of their way to help relieve human suffering even when it inconveniences them, the child is inclined to accept this as a moral value—it is good to show compassion to others. Elder suggests that parents model such moral values as:

respect	fair play
kindness to others	clean bodies
love for God	forgiving attitude
love for people	responsibility
hard work	faithfulness

Fundamental to this list of modeled values is honesty and trust.[10]

Ann Landers recently included a letter in her newspaper column which illustrates this need for implicit guidance to be given through parental models. A mother wrote:

Dear Ann: I had an experience recently with my 16-year-old that is worth sharing. We were shopping and she selected a shirt and vest priced at $15.95. We found a blouse that matched for $9.95. She put the three pieces together and said, "I'll bet we can get the three pieces for $15.95." I said nothing. Sure enough, the woman rang up $15.95 and began to wrap the merchandise.

I stopped her and said, "You made a mistake. The blouse was extra." The woman was very grateful and thanked me. When we got outside my daughter said, "That was dumb of you." I did not respond.

As soon as we got home she went to the phone and called her best friend to say how neat it was—what her Mom had done. Then she came into the kitchen and thanked me and said, "I'll never try anything crooked again. I would not have enjoyed wearing that stolen blouse."

So, if any of you parents out there wonder what goes on inside your kids' heads, take my word for it. They are looking to you for an example of decent behavior and when they don't get it they're let down.[11]

In addition, however, character development is dependent upon explicit guidance given through instruction and discussion of moral issues. In light of the conflicting moral standards existing in contemporary society, parents must also be alert to using the daily experiences of the child as an occasion for direct teaching.

Television programs and newscasts, school activities, newsstand reading material, and casual conversation all affect character formation for good or bad. Parents can take advantage of these experiences for discussing right or wrong attitudes toward self and others. This type of guidance is suggested by the word translated "instruction" (Eph. 6:4). It has the meaning of warning or admonition and therefore suggests explicit teaching.

In the Mixed Marriage
(1 Cor. 7:12–16; 1 Pet. 3:1–2)

The final marital relationship to which we give attention is not discussed in the Ephesians passage since Paul was addressing the Christian family in that context. But in Paul's day, as in ours, the question of how to deal with marriages in which one mate is a Christian and the other not was a subject of concern. Paul did speak directly to this issue in 1 Corinthians 7, and Peter instructed the wife in such a marriage in chapter 3 of his first letter. Let us consider some of the implications of these two passages.

Accept the validness of the marriage in God's grace. Paul and Peter responded to situations created by one mate becoming a Christian after the marriage was already in existence. The issue, therefore, is not whether a Christian should marry an unbeliever but whether the convert should remain in the marriage and if so, how to respond to the unbelieving mate. The apostle Paul was very emphatic in his affirmation that the mixed marriage is a valid marriage for the believer. He declared that "the unbelieving husband is consecrated through her husband. Otherwise, your children would be unclean, but as it is they are holy" (1 Cor. 7:14). Since the marriage is a valid one, the believer should not take any initiative to dissolve the marriage as long as the unbeliever is willing to maintain it.

Practice one's Christian faith in the home. In his instruction to the Christian wife, Peter encouraged the same type of voluntary yieldedness in love that Paul described in Ephesians as essential to Christian marriage. The wife is to show her authentic faith by the manner in which she lives her daily life with the unbelieving husband. The very center of her selfhood is to be revealed in her "gentle and quiet spirit, which in God's sight is very precious" (1 Pet. 3:4).

In Peter's day the unbelieving mate was more apt to be a man rather than a woman so his message is addressed directly to the Christian wife. While this is still true today, we know that there are many men whose wives are unbelievers, and the man is challenged to let his authentic Christian selfhood be revealed in the way that he demonstrates Christian love to his wife.

One objective of walking in love as Christ has loved us is that the unbelieving mate may be influenced to accept Christ as personal Savior because of the example given by the believing mate. This type of evangelistic witness is considered to be more influential than a nagging, critical attitude toward the unbeliever. Husbands or wives married to non-Christian mates can be helped to understand the importance of this attitude in our contemporary situation.

It is also obvious that this kind of daily witness is different from the advice to use one's feminine sexuality as a means for influencing the husband to become a Christian! This can be manipulation of the mate whereas Peter was describing authentic love in practice.

Accept the fact of marital breakup if the unbelieving mate will not stay in the marriage. (1 Cor. 7:15–16). In Paul's word to the mixed marriage, he acknowledged that he had no direct teaching from the Lord since we have no record of Jesus dealing with this issue. However, Paul had no hesitancy in offering an interpretation of what the believer should do in the light of Christian faith. He said, "But if the unbelieving partner desires to separate, let it be so; in such a case the brother or sister is not bound" (1 Cor. 7:15). Dwight Hervey Small is probably right when he says that "Paul offers them reassurance that cannot possibly set very well today with a multitude of evangelical pastors in the land! Paul says that in such instances the Christian is not to fight it, not to try everything possible to keep the marriage together. Paul is a bit more realistic than many pastors in this regard. He elevates personal peace above the retention of the mere formality of marriage."[12] The term translated "not bound" was a legal term that could refer to freeing a slave, divorcing a mate, or freeing one from a contractual obligation. Interpreters differ as to the implication of this term for marriage, but it seems clear that Paul was telling the Corinthian Christians that they were free from the marital contract in a total way. Therefore, it is assumed that Paul was saying the believer is free to enter into a new marital relationship without penalty since the old marriage was dissolved completely. The basic reason for such a divorce was expressed by Paul in his statement that "God has called us to peace" (1 Cor. 7:15). The Christian is reminded that in some situations no amount of Christian witness will convert the unbelieving partner, and it is better to dissolve the relationship than to live in constant turmoil over the mixed-marriage situation.

This admonition of Paul is contained in a chapter of a letter that many believe cannot be generalized to all Christians because of the particular problems of the Corinthian community. Whether his advice to the religiously mixed marriage should be made a general teaching of the church is subject, therefore, to serious deliberation. One thing is certain, Paul had strong convictions that marriage should be a permanent relationship according to Christ's teachings, but he was perfectly willing to make a situational judgment that permitted divorce under certain circumstances. This at least gives biblical warrant for the belief that individual circumstances do influence how the ethical ideas of the Bible are to be applied to decision making on a particular issue such as divorce.

Small interprets the intent of the Pauline instruction to mean that peace in marital relationships is a fundamental principle of the grace relationship. He declares, "What is this but an indirect way of saying that the essence of true marriage is peace, and that a destructively conflicted marriage is sometimes not worth trying to save if one partner is not a Christian."[13]

It is my conviction that Paul's advice in Corinthians illustrates the continuing tension between ethical ideal and pastoral concern that is true of the entire New Testament. Marriage for keeps is a biblical ideal, but persons are not to be sacrificed to the ideal if it destroys other values of human personhood at the same time.

It seems to me that we are dealing with an issue very similar to the issue concerning the proper use of the sabbath that

Jesus confronted with the Pharisees. The Old Testament commanded that the sabbath be kept holy and that remunerative work not be done on the sabbath. During New Testament times the rabbinical literature had developed a strict set of rules concerning the way in which the sabbath should be kept. As Jesus and his disciples walked through grainfields on the sabbath, they broke off some of the ears of grain and ate them. The Jewish leaders accused them of threshing on the sabbath and thereby breaking the law.

In Jesus' answer to their accusation, he reminded them that their Scriptures contained the story of David breaking the ritual law by eating the ceremonial bread in the Temple when he and his followers were hungry. And then Jesus said to them, "The sabbath was made for man, not man for the sabbath; so the Son of man is lord even of the sabbath" (Mark 2:27–28).

There is no doubt that the sabbath was divinely ordered in the Ten Commandments, but its purpose was for man's welfare. Marriage is also a divinely ordained relationship, and it is for man's welfare (Gen. 2:18–24). If maintaining the ideal of marriage becomes destructive to the moral and spiritual well-being of the persons involved in it, the principle of lifelong marriage may have to be sacrificed to the interests of the principle of human well-being. Marriage is made for man, not man for marriage. This seems to be implicit in Paul's instructions to the believers in Corinth whose unbelieving mates desired divorce rather than marriage.

Throughout this chapter we have focused on describing how the concept of submission as "yieldedness in love" is expected of all family members in their relationship to each other. Questions have probably come to your mind concerning the actual application of this principle to the development of family relations. The final chapter of the book will be devoted to this discussion, but first it is important to discuss some of the essential qualities of personal life in the family.

If the home is Christian, how does Christian faith express itself in the personal attitudes and emotions of the family members?

Notes

1. Letha Scanzoni and Nancy Hardesty, *All We're Meant to Be*, p. 51.

2. Ibid., p. 43.

3. Ray Summers, *Ephesians: Pattern for Christian Living*, p. 123.

4. Reprinted with permission of Macmillan Publishing Co., Inc. from J. B. Phillips: *The New Testament in Modern English,* Revised Edition. © J. B. Phillips 1958, 1960, 1972. Subsequent quotations are marked Phillips.

5. Paul Tournier, *To Understand Each Other,* trans. John S. Gilmour (Richmond: John Knox Press, 1970), p. 28.

6. W. Wayne Grant, *Growing Parents Growing Children* (Nashville: Convention Press, 1977), p. 95.

7. Ibid., p. 56.

8. Ibid., p. 102.

9. Carl A. Elder, *Values and Moral Development in Children* (Nashville: Broadman Press, 1976), p. 41.

10. Ibid., p. 42.

11. *Kansas City Times,* February 2, 1978, p. 70.

12. Dwight Hervey Small, *The Right to Remarry* (Old Tappan, New Jersey: Fleming H. Revell Co., 1977), p. 167.

13. Ibid., p. 169.

V
Quality of Relationship in the Home

Now that we have examined the patterns of relationship that should characterize the Christian home in its practice of mutual submission, let us consider the basic qualities of these relationships as expressed in the teachings of the Gospels as well as in the letters to the churches.

Authentic Love
(Rom. 12:9–10; 1 Cor. 13:4–7; Eph. 5:1–2,25; Col. 3:14; Titus 2:5; Matt. 22:35–40)

In his letter to the Roman Christians, Paul emphasized the nature of the love that is to be expressed between Christians when he said, "Let love be genuine," or as Phillips translates it, "Let us have no imitation Christian love" (Rom. 12:9).

Arthur Rouner has a delightful little book entitled *How to Love . . .* in which he rightly acknowledges that love is a very vague and general term which is hard to define. He indicates, though, that love "is a word, a quality, and a reality of frightening power. And if we do not somehow learn to understand it, use it, and grow with it, all our relationships are in peril."[1]

The quality of authentic love is foundational to the understanding of the interpersonal relationships which have been analyzed in our discussion of the patterns of relationships in the Christian marriage. Since love is certainly "a many splendored thing" with varying shades of meanings, let us consider some applications of love to the Christian family situation.

Love as Attraction: Eros. The Greek word *eros* is not used in the New Testament as a descriptive term for love, but it is used in the Greek translation of the Old Testament called the Septuagint. The word was originally used in Greek philosophy to describe a person's consecration to the search for and possession of beauty and good in an ethical sense. Later in Greek thought it developed the connotation of possessing another person sexually and thus became a common term for sexual desire. In the Septuagint it was used to translate such phrases as "I am my beloved's, and his desire is for me" from the Song of Solomon (v. 10). Therefore it did suggest the attraction of sexual possessiveness.

Even though the term does not appear in the New Testament writings, sexual love is one aspect of the authentic love which binds husband and wife into the unity of one flesh. Sexual relationships for the Christian couple are to be physically pleasurable and symbolic in a deeper sense of the commitment and fidelity of the marital union. The authors of *Equal Marriage* are right on target in their affirmation, "We don't believe there is any room for sexual experiments with other partners in a good marriage." But they are just as firm in their conclusion that "a marriage without adequate sex begins to unravel."[2] The meaning of adequacy will be determined by different couples in different ways, but eros love is a part of authentic love. It is the attractive, sexual dimension of a growing marriage that for many couples does last throughout their lives together.

Love as Friendship: Philia. Philia is love as personal warmth, affection, and responsiveness. The Greeks also had the word *storge* describing natural affection between persons. Paul, in Romans 12:10, used a combination form of these two words when he instructed the believers to "love one another with brotherly affection." He is encouraging a tender, affectionate love between them which can properly be called friendship. Even though the apostle was actually addressing the church fellowship in this passage of Scripture, his instruction is just as relevant to the home. Love in the family should be a friendship kind of love.

Lois Wyse, in her *Love Poems for the Very Married,* has a beautifully written expression of love as friendship.

> Someone asked me
> To name the time
> Our friendship stopped
> And love began.
> Oh, my darling
> That's the secret.
> Our friendship
> Never stopped.[3]

In contrast, however, some marriages and families have not discovered love as friendship. During a state family-life conference, Dr. Dale Cowling, pastor of the Second Baptist Church in Little Rock, Arkansas, was a program personality. In his presentation he remarked, "As a pastor it disturbs me to see the number of couples who say they *love* each other but they don't seem to *like* each other." This apparent contradiction in terms is clarified by Samuel Southard in his book *Like the One You Love.* Southard says that couples making this kind of impression usually distinguish love from like in this way: "Like is the enjoyment in doing things together, in mutual respect, and in fulfillment. 'Love' is more connected to sentimentality, sexual attraction, the giving and receiving of affection."[4] In his book he points out that marital relationships which blend both liking and loving are a desirable goal for marriage. "When the two come together," Southard maintains, "we have a new form of love, one in which erotic fulfillment and responsibility for children are fused with the response of equals to mutually satisfying goals."[5]

Even though Southard limits the target audience for his book to middle-class people who are looking for a partnership form of marriage, his insights into love as friendship are helpful to any Christian marriage. It requires of us the willingness to act toward our mate and children with the same considerateness we would practice in our relationships with friends. We can seek to fulfill the Scripture which says, "A friend loves at all times" (Prov. 17:17).

Love as Unselfish Caring: Agape. The word *agape* has become a familiar term in our contemporary culture. Young people have celebrated their understanding of it in *agape* fellowships, churches have established *agape* houses for ministering to youth, and pastors have incorporated it into their sermons on love. The lexicons define it as kindly concern, redemptive concern, generosity, devotedness, valuing another, and faithfulness. In our discussion of family love, we use it to describe the unselfish love which serves others through voluntary self-giving. It is an act of voluntary choice rather than an expression of emotional response.

In Ephesians 5:25, the Christian husband is instructed to love his wife in this manner. In Colossians 3:14, it is this kind of love which "binds everything together in perfect harmony." It is the kind of love which took Jesus to a cross for the salvation of lost persons.

A contemporary definition of *love* by the American psychiatrist Harry Stack Sullivan offers a practical means for testing one's understanding of *agape* in interpersonal relations: "When the satisfaction or the security of another person becomes as significant to one as is one's own satisfaction or security, then the state of love exists."[6]

A sixteen-year-old girl gave an excellent illustration of *agape* during a family-life conference in her church. "When I was fifteen," she said, "I wanted everything in our family to revolve around me. I wanted my own way regardless of what the other family members wanted, and I was hard to live with if I did not get my way. Then I went on a Youth retreat where the leader talked about love as unselfishness. I began to see myself as a selfish person but I did nothing to change. Our church had a Youth revival later on, and I became more aware that my attitude was wrong. I rededicated my life to Christ during the revival and asked him to help me change. It has not been easy but I have found that our home life is much happier now that I am more concerned for others' needs in our family." She had discovered that unselfish love is more Christian and more fulfilling than selfishness, even though it was not always easy.

As Arthur Rouner indicates, *agape* love is

very different from good feelings. And very different from tremors in the tummy. And very different from endless good times and from sexual fun and games. The test of love is suffering, enduring difficulty, putting up with problems, and letting someone else's life be more important than your own.[7]

Authentic love, therefore, is a combination of continuing attraction to each other, warm feelings of friendship with each other, and willing self-giving for each other. Its qualities are summed up beautifully by Paul:

Love is patient and kind; love is not jealous or boastful; it is not arrogant or rude. Love does not insist on its own way; it is not irritable or resentful; it does not rejoice at wrong, but rejoices in the right. Love bears all things, believes all things, hopes all things, endures all things. Love never ends (1 Cor. 13:4–8).

Love as the Gift of God. If our minds and hearts are staggered by the challenge of living authentically in love when we know our limitations and weaknesses as human beings, we can take heart by hearing the New Testament writers tell us that such love is one of God's gifts to his children.

In 1 John 4:19, the apostle reminds us that our capacity to love is given by the One who is love: "We love, because he first loved us." When we put on Christ in faith, we come into personal contact with the source of love in our lives.

Paul, in Galatians 5:5–6, helps us understand that faith and love are in close relationship in the believer's life: "For in Christ

Jesus neither circumcision nor uncircumcision is of any avail, but faith working through love" (v. 6).

But perhaps the most encouraging promise of Scripture is that "the fruit of the Spirit is love, joy, peace, patience, kindness, goodness, faithfulness, gentleness, self control" (Gal. 5:22–23) and that by the power of the indwelling Holy Spirit of God we can develop into better lovers! As we voluntarily yield our lives to the Spirit's control, we will become more like the One who sent the Spirit to dwell in our midst. As we have said earlier, the voluntary yieldedness of our lives to one another is an act of love reflecting the Spirit-filled life. God's own Spirit helps us love as we ought.

Shared Joy
(Eph. 5:19–20; Gal. 5:22; Phil. 4:4)

A group of girls in a missionary organization were asked, What is the most important desire you have for your family to experience together? After some discussion the girls agreed that their greatest desire was to have a happy home where people enjoyed one another.

Joy is a fundamental quality of Christian living. The Old Testament describes joy in terms of purely social experiences as well as the highest joy one found in worshiping God in the tabernacle or Temple. The New Testament witness records the great joy of the Wise Men who saw the star as well as the message of joy which greeted the wondering shepherds in the fields on that first Christmas night. The New Testament message celebrates the joy of living as God's gift to mankind. As Paul affirmed, joy is a fruit of the Spirit. It is life in which singing and thanksgiving flow forth from hearts made new in grace.

Yet the truth is that many Christian families do not live in the joy of their Christian faith. Their homes witness more tears and harsh words than sounds of laughter. Small arguments become grave crises because there is no sense of humor which enables a family member to laugh at self and with others. It is not an exaggeration to affirm that the ability to laugh at oneself and to demonstrate joy in relationship is fundamental to marital and family happiness.

The writer of Ecclesiastes reflected many human misconceptions of what the good life really is in his brief writing, but one phrase needs to be echoed over and over again to people in our generation: "Enjoy life with the wife whom you love" (9:9). Love and joy are to be shared experiences of the Christian home.

In the ancient wisdom of Proverbs can be found two choice reminders of the value of shared joy in the family: "A cheerful heart is a good medicine,/but a downcast spirit dries up the bones" (17:22); "A glad heart makes a cheerful countenance,/ but by sorrow of heart the spirit is broken" (15:13). This kind of joy and happiness is discovered through the releasing of one's life to the everpresent Spirit of God who gives us joy in heart. There is a certain note of abandonment in it which finds life to be fun as well as joyous. Perhaps more couples need to share the reported story of one young couple's search for happiness.

The young husband had read all of the psychological and religious self-help books on marriage, personal adjustment, and the total man that he could find. His wife had tried to live up to all the glorious expectations of these writings to please her husband. But one day her rebellion was clearly expressed: "Now that we've found real happiness, couldn't we have some fun, too?"

In the *Journal of Katherine Mansfield* is this delightful word: "To be wildly enthusiastic or deadly serious—both are wrong. Both pass . . . . But the sense of humor I have found of use in every single occasion of my life."[8]

Shared joy in the family includes having fun and enjoying

laughter, telling jokes and acting silly, experiencing the deep joy of a full moon on a snow-covered landscape, and rejoicing in the Lord always (Phil. 4:4).

Mutual Respect
(Eph. 5:33; Rom. 12:10; 1 Cor. 12:4–26)

As Paul summarized the mutual responsibilities of the husband-wife relationship in Ephesians 5, he reminded the husband that he is to love his wife and the wife that she is to respect her husband (v. 33). Respect is thus identified as one of the essential qualities of family relationships just as it is expected to be demonstrated in all walks of life for the Christian.

Mutual respect is essential in Christian faith (Rom. 12:10; 1 Cor. 12:14–26). We have already given consideration to the first part of Romans 12:10 where Paul told the body of Christ to be tenderly affectionate to one another. In the second part of the verse he encouraged them to "outdo one another in showing honor." The believers are to practice the Christian grace of respect for each other if the body of Christ is to live in the harmony for which Christ intended it. This same principle of mutual respect is treated more fully in 1 Corinthians 12 where Paul discussed the importance of each individual's gifts to the total ministry of the fellowship. After affirming the Holy Spirit as the common source of these gifts and as the unifying principle of the church's fellowship, Paul pointed out the necessity of respecting each other's gifts since all are necessary for the church to do its work. He said the members are to care deeply for one another because "if one member suffers, all suffer together; if one member is honored, all rejoice together" (1 Cor. 12:26). The unity of the body is dependent upon mutually respecting one another.

Mutual respect is vital in family unity. The family is like the church in that each person has his own personality style and distinctive gifts to share. Acceptance of the instruction to be submissive to each other is dependent upon the kind of respect for one another that makes submission a voluntary act of love rather than a forced response to dominant authority.

Respecting one another as persons rather than treating each other as things or objects begins early in life. Dr. Wayne Grant told a summer conference group that in his work as a pediatrician he had come to believe that mutual respect is one of the most basic qualities necessary for Christian child rearing. This principle is reinforced in his book for parents where he says: "The relationship between the Christian parent and child should be based upon the same mutual respect that Christ taught man to show in all personal relationships."[9] In the parent-child relationship: "The best way to teach a child respect is to practice on him. If he has your respect, it will be a natural thing for him to show respect to others."[10] Parents often demand respect from their children but do not give the same respect to their children. A child's self-image may be seriously damaged by parents who use ridicule or sarcasm in correcting their child's mistakes.

A married woman with grown children came to a Christian counseling center for help in overcoming very negative feelings about her worth as a person. During the counseling she revealed that her father had continually told her, "You are stupid" whenever she made any of the normal mistakes that children make in growing up. She had so internalized this belief in her stupidity that now as an adult she was still struggling to overcome the emotional damage done to her. Parental lack of respect for her as a child had made it almost impossible for her to respect herself and to feel comfortable about other people.

Mutual respect is also an important part of the parent-young person relationship during the stresses of the adolescent period. Since trust is so intimately related to respect, we could say that one is really the flip side of the other and both are essential. Youth needs to feel trusted and parents need to be respected. But respect is difficult to maintain if trust is consistently broken.

The Christian family needs to be able to express the mutual respect which is based upon accepted trust as well.

A father and his fifteen-year-old son, who had qualified for his driving permit, were practicing driving one Sunday afternoon when a carload of young people drove past them.

"Look, Dad," said Bill, "There goes Jim in his parent's car. He doesn't even have a permit, and he is driving their car while they are out of town."

The father thought for a moment and then said, "You know, Bill, I really can't conceive of you taking our car out like that while we were away from home."

"Why not," responded Bill, "everybody does it."

That Sunday night the family attended the evening service of their church's family-life conference. The message happened to focus on the need for mutual respect in the home as one essential quality of interpersonal relations.

As the people left the church following the service, Bill caught up with his dad and exclaimed, "I know now why you would not expect me to take the car while you were away."

"Why?" questioned the father.

"Because in our home we respect each other!" was Bill's immediate reply. He had recognized how vital was the family's trust and respect for each other, and he knew he would not want to destroy that important relationship.

Mutual respect is also essential to a marriage in which equality of personhood is to be honored. I am convinced that authentic love can never be fully realized unless couples have a deep sense of honest respect for each other. In *Equal Marriage*, the authors declare that "more than anything else, equal marriage is an attitude—one of mutual respect."[11] Because many men in our society grow up feeling that females are in some way inferior to males, it is often difficult for a man to respect his wife as a fully equal person. When such a man is able to honestly confront this feeling in himself and allow the Holy Spirit to implant an attitude of Christian equality of persons in his heart, he will be able to respect his wife in a new way. On the other hand the wife must be able to respect her husband and be a woman worthy of his respect if this is to happen. Only then can a companionship or partnership marriage become a reality.

In my experience as pastor and marriage counselor, I have seldom (if ever) seen a woman struggle with the authority problem in marriage if she respected her husband completely and felt that he also respected her. Mutual respect is essential to wholesome Christian family living.

Expressed Forgiveness
(Eph. 4:32; Col. 3:12; Matt. 6:14–15)

Two of the most difficult phrases for many people to say are, "I'm sorry," and "I forgive you." Yet in Christian family life these sentences characterize the means of renewed relationship when difficulties and problems arise. Forgiveness is the oil that lubricates the friction of closeness in the daily routine of the home. When freely expressed, it permits us to remain close without continually heating up the emotions of rejection and resentment. In the New Testament, forgiveness is a fundamental quality of life.

To forgive another is to practice the forgiveness we have received from Christ. In Ephesians 1:7, Paul gave testimony to God's gift of grace through Jesus Christ in whom "we have redemption through his blood, the forgiveness of our trespasses, according to the riches of his grace which he has lavished upon us." Our personal pathway to salvation was made possible through the forgiveness we experienced from the Father when we confessed our sins and accepted Christ as our Savior and Lord. Whereas we had been among those "dead through the trespasses and sins in which [we] once walked, following the course of this world . . . and so we were by nature children of wrath" (Eph. 2:1–3), our trespasses have been forgiven, and we are now saved to walk in newness of life. Praise God for his gracious gift of forgiveness!

Yes, but praising God for what we have received is inadequate if we do not incarnate the forgiving spirit into our own hearts and offer the grace of forgiveness to those who hurt us either deliberately or unintentionally. Our Lord told a scathing parable about a forgiven debtor who refused to be forgiving to others (Matt. 18:23–35). After describing the judgment which came upon the unforgiving servant, he said, "So also my heavenly Father will do to every one of you, if you do not forgive your brother from your heart" (v. 35). The judgment sounds harsh to our ears, but it symbolizes how seriously Christ felt about his disciples practicing forgiveness in their human relationships.

After teaching the prayer which we call the Lord's Prayer including the petition, "Forgive us our debts, as we forgive our debtors" (Matt. 6:12, KJV), Jesus added, "For if you forgive men their trespasses, your heavenly Father also will forgive you; but if you do not forgive men their trespasses, neither will your Father forgive your trespasses" (Matt. 6:14–15). This sounds like legalistic heavenly bookkeeping, but I am convinced that this was not the intent of the statement. It seems to me that Jesus is clearly telling us that if we cannot offer forgiveness to others, we are really incapable of accepting it for ourselves. Only the forgiven know how to be truly forgiving. This we must do if we are to incarnate our own forgiveness into life. Paul emphasized this when he said we are to be "forgiving one another, as God in Christ forgave you" (Eph. 4:32).

To forgive is to clear the air of hostility. Samuel Southard makes the interesting observation that "strong love depends on clean memories" and "much of marriage counseling is a cleaning operation."[12] The counselor is trying to help the couple clean out the elements of hate and disappointment that pollute the air of their life space in the family. We are well aware of the potential destruction that air pollution can cause in our major cities, but we may not have recognized how hate pollution and disappointment pollution from the past can destroy our present life in human relations. Forgiveness is the cleansing agent which can clear the air of hostility in the home.

Forgiveness is needed when cruel and cutting words have been flung at mate or children or parents.

Forgiveness is needed when trust has been broken by the deliberate desire to deceive.

Forgiveness is needed when selfishness has caused us to ride roughshod over the rights of others in the home.

Forgiveness is needed when pregnancy is a reality for our unmarried daughter.

Forgiveness is needed when buried resentments toward parents are blocking our ability to love them in their aging years.

Forgiveness is needed when the spiritual cancer called hate is destroying our own peace with self and with God.

Forgiveness is the way to clean up the air pollution in our home life which can ultimately destroy our families or separate us from each other so completely that we live in a vacuum of aloneness.

To forgive is to open the way to reconciliation (Rom. 5:9–11). Hurt feelings and unresolved anger have a way of separating people from each other. Even while lying close together in a bed with bodies touching, marital partners have felt the wall of separation that kept them from turning toward one another in tender expressions of love. These barriers are also felt between parent and child when disappointments have caused anguish and pain. Anger at one's self and feelings of rejection from other family members can add additional rows of bricks to the wall of separation that forces us farther and farther away from the intimacy we long to experience. Even between friends at church there can be experiences of rejection which drive us away from love and into the loneliness of self-pity and resentment.

In a Southern Baptist hospital the chaplain was requested by a medical doctor to call on a patient. The lady had no physical illness which the doctor could discover, but she was wasting away with some kind of psychosomatic problem he could not uncover. She had refused to seek counseling help so he hospitalized her and asked the chaplain to see what he could do to penetrate her depression.

As the chaplain visited with the patient, she said, "Chaplain, I just feel like God is far away on the other side of a wall and I can't get to him anymore." Then, little by little, the story unfolded. She had been organist in her church for many years when new leadership came into prominence in the church's organizational life. In a way that may have been unkind or simply mishandled, she was relieved of her job as organist. From that time on she began to nurse feelings of rejection and anger which she could not overcome, and her body began to show the effects of her buried hostility. She would not forgive those who had hurt her so much.

Recognizing her problem, the chaplain said, "You may feel that you cannot get over the wall of separation that blocks your way to God. But if you are willing, God can get over that wall to you and then break down the wall completely." She understood what he was saying—be willing to forgive those who have hurt you and you can be healed, spiritually and physically. But her bitterness had become too much a part of her; she refused reconciliation because she refused to forgive. She could not follow the steps outlined in Paul's letter to the Romans—to go from justification or forgiveness to reconciliation to joy (Rom. 5:8–11). Yet there is the promise of the gospel for our relationships to God and to one another.

Expressed and accepted forgiveness is the means by which barriers are broken down and reconciliation takes place. Then the joy of living and loving together can be restored once more. Whether the issue is one of recent occasion or one that has clouded our relationship for a long time, forgiveness is the pathway to reconciliation.

Accepted Grace
(Eph. 2:8–10; 4:2,7; 1 Pet. 3:7; 1 Cor. 15:10)

The young adults of the church had gathered in the fellowship hall on a Saturday morning for a one-day marriage enrichment retreat. Among the sixteen couples was one young man and woman who had been married only three months. Her shyness was apparent as the retreat activities began, but she and her husband entered fully into the program. One of the assignments given by the retreat leader was for each individual to write out his own answers to this statement: These are the things you do that make me know you love me, honor me, value me, respect me. Then the large group was divided into groups of four couples each. Within the small groups, each couple was to read aloud to each other the statements written on the paper while seated in chairs facing one another.

The young wife started to read, began to cry, then brushed away her tears with a determination to go on. As part of her words to her husband she said, "I know you love me because you took me to be your wife when I did not deserve to be. I am not good enough for you but you love me anyhow."

Whether her assessment of her own worth was accurate is not our concern. The point is that she felt unworthy but was loved in spite of her feelings of unworthiness. To this extent she was a recipient of accepted grace and her life was changed because of it. This is the meaning of grace.

Paul affirmed, "By grace you have been saved through faith; and this is not your own doing, it is the gift of God" (Eph. 2:8). He also declared that "grace was given to each of us according to the measure of Christ's gift" (Eph. 4:7) and "by the grace of God I am what I am, and his grace toward me was not in vain" (1 Cor. 15:10). In Paul's life, accepted grace led him to conversion, new life, and apostleship. In our lives, accepted grace can also bring us through salvation to a new life in which the grace of God's love is expressed through us to others. Peter added an additional note when he reminded the Christian husband and wife that they "are joint heirs of the grace of life" (1 Pet. 3:7).

Bible dictionaries point out that grace and love are so closely related it is often difficult to distinguish one from the other in Christian life. For our own purpose, however, we will let love *(agape)* signify the freely offered gift of salvation made possible by the cross, and grace *(karis)* symbolize the acceptance which God extends to us when we respond to his offer of redemptive love.

Grace is acceptance. The Clinebells are so right when they say:

Fortunate is the couple in whose relationship there is something which allows them both to experience grace—the accepting love which one does not need to earn because it is present as a spontaneous expression of the relationship.[13]

Paul seemed to have something like this in mind when he said we are to be "forbearing one another in love" (Eph. 4:2). An interpretive translation of this verse might read, "putting up with what you've got in love!" Obviously, however, there are family situations in which the behavior of one person toward others may be so destructive that continuing acceptance of the behavior would be wrong and could be disastrous. A student came to see me one day to discuss the problem situation of a member of his church. The woman was married to a violent man who would beat her when he came home drunk. She was afraid to remain with him but also afraid to leave him. Finally she was willing to consider a divorce but felt this was wrong for her as a Christian. The student pastor had not worked through his own attitude toward divorce and could give her little help. Even after our conversation about divorce, he did not feel he could be supportive to her desire to leave her husband.

Several months later the student returned to my office to tell me that the husband had come home in a violent, ugly mood and had stabbed his wife to death. No amount of expressed grace on her part was able to change the sin-filled heart of her husband. Acceptance in situations of physical abuse of wife or children should not be tolerated without getting help for the offender.

In the normal situation of family living, however, acceptance of the individual in love even when the behavior is wrong is to live out our own experience of acceptance with Christ.

Grace is renewal. You may have voiced on many occasions the desire of the poet who wrote:

> I wish that there were some wonderful place
>   Called the Land of Beginning Again,
> Where all our mistakes and all our heartaches,
>   And all of our poor selfish grief
> Could be dropped like a shabby old coat at the door
>   And never put on again.
>
> —Louise Fletcher Tarkington

The New Testament affirmation is that we are able to be renewed into God's handiwork by accepting the grace of God through faith and placing our lives in his renewing power. Paul's testimony, "By the grace of God I am what I am, and his grace toward me was not in vain" (1 Cor. 15:10), can be ours if we are willing to offer our lives to the One who can renew us. Individual family members and the family itself can have a renewal experience as God's grace is appropriated in family relations.

Some years ago *Home Life* magazine carried the story of a woman who was being honored by her Woman's Missionary Union circle as an outstanding example of authentic Christian womanhood. When she began her response to this significant honor, she said, "Would you be surprised to learn that my life was changed by a tramp?" The women waited in eager expectation to hear the story.

During the depression years of the early 1930s my husband was fortunate enough to have a job at a time when many others did not. One day a tramp came to my back door to ask for food. He offered to work for it, but I would have nothing to do with him. I gave him a tongue lashing for being a beggar and finally told him to get away from my door or I would call my husband.

"Your husband is not home," he said quietly.

"How do you know?" I answered in astonishment.

"Well, if he is home it is only because he is sick. Nobody would stay home with a tongue like yours if he could get away!" The tramp turned, walked down the walk, and was gone.

I leaned against the door frame of my back door and said, "Lord, is that really the kind of person I am?" Then I remembered when my husband left for work that morning. I had not walked with him down the walk, I had talked him down the walk, and it had been critical all the way. As I reflected on this experience, I prayed, "Lord, if you will help me, I am going to change. I am going to try to be the kind of Christian person that you want me to be." Whatever you see in my life now is the result of God's renewing grace that changed me and my life in the home.

Accepted grace is, therefore, accepting one's self as a person of worth, accepting others in the family in a way that accentuates their selfhood, and accepting the renewing power of God's Spirit in our daily life.

Continuing Growth
(Eph. 4:15–16; Phil. 1:9–11; Col. 1:9–12)

In our relationship with our Lord, the gospel accepts us where we are, but it does not leave us there. The Christian life is to be one of dynamic growth in which "we are to grow up in every way into him who is the head, into Christ" (Eph. 4:15). Paul also prayed that Christians will experience a relationship in which "your love may abound more and more, with knowledge and all discernment" (Phil. 1:9) in order that you may know how to choose wisely in the important issues of life. The New Testament is growth oriented, and the inspired writers often rebuke Christians for not continuing to grow after accepting Christ as their Savior.

Marriages and families should also experience growth as we move through the changing cycles of family life. Because our relationships are personal, the growth process is neither automatic nor always upward. For most marriages, there are peaks of enrichment, plateaus of routineness, and valleys of despair as we experience the normal joys and crises of family living. Overall, however, the family experience can be one in which continuing growth does occur.

But growth does not happen without effort. The David Maces speak from over forty years of marriage counseling experience when they point out that "the development of a really good marriage is not a natural process. It is an achievement."[14] One of the essential qualities of a good marriage and a rewarding family life is to continue to grow in love, in understanding, in acceptance, in forgiveness, and in creative ways of maintaining the vitality of the relationship.

Here, then, are some essential qualities of relationship in the Christian home: *authentic love, shared joy, mutual respect, expressed forgiveness, accepted grace,* and *continuing growth.* When the patterns of family interaction are infused with these qualities, life in the home can be rich, rewarding, and joyous. The Spirit of the living Christ will truly be living with us in such a family.

Notes

1. Arthur A. Rouner, *How to Love . . .* (Grand Rapids: Baker Book House, 1974), p. 11.

2. Jean Stapleton and Richard Bright, *Equal Marriage* (Nashville: Abingdon Press, 1976), pp. 40–41.

3. Quoted in *The Intimate Marriage* by Howard J. and Charlotte H. Clinebell, p. 23.

4. Samuel Southard, *Like the One You Love* (Philadelphia: Westminster Press, 1974), p. 12.

5. Ibid.

6. Harry Stack Sullivan, *Conceptions of Modern Psychiatry* (New York: W. W. Norton and Co., Inc., 1953), pp. 42–43.

7. Rouner, p. 15.

8. Quoted in *A Reader's Notebook,* ed. Gerald Kennedy (New York: Harper and Bros., 1953), p. 133.

9. W. Wayne Grant, *Growing Parents Growing Children,* p. 19.

10. Ibid., p. 90

11. Stapleton and Bright, p. 17.

12. Southard, pp. 49, 51.

13. Clinebell, p. 186.

14. David and Vera Mace, *We Can Have Better Marriages If We Really Want Them* (Nashville: Abingdon Press, 1974), p. 11.

VI

Developing Your Own Marriage Style

Now that we have given attention to the meaning of mutual equality and submissiveness in biblical perspective, let us examine how Christian couples may integrate these principles into their own marriages. My purpose in this chapter is to discuss the development of the family in contemporary culture, to review some of the styles for marriage recommended in popular literature, and to offer suggestions for creative development of a growing Christian marriage.

Development of the Family

In 1945 two widely known sociologists published a study of the American family which became a classic in the field of family sociology. Ernest W. Burgess and Harvey J. Locke named their book, *The Family: From Institution to Companionship.* In the introduction they described the fundamental principle which they had discovered in their intensive study of family life in the United States, as well as in some other countries. "The central thesis of this volume," wrote Burgess and Locke, "is that the family in historical times has been, and at present is, in transition from an institution to a companionship." A rather lengthy quote will help us understand what they mean by the terms *institution* and *companionship.*

In the past the important factors unifying the family have been external, formal, and authoritarian, as the law, the mores, public opinion, tradition, the authority of the family head, rigid discipline, and elaborate ritual. At present, in the new emerging form of the companionship family, its unity inheres less and less in community pressures and more and more in such interpersonal relations in the mutual affection; the sympathetic understanding and the comradeship of its members.[1]

As Burgess and Locke reviewed the history of family styles, they described three basic types of family relationships. The first was *the large patriarchal family of ancient society* in which "the patriarch exercises more or less absolute control over his wife, his unmarried daughters, and his sons and their wives and children."[2] The family styles of the ancient Romans, Greeks, and Hebrews were largely patterned in this style; in the Hebrew patriarchal family, the absolute authority of the father was tempered somewhat by the Mosaic law.

The development of the industrial revolution in the Middle Ages led to the second family style, that of the *small patriarchal family.* Dominance of the male head, whether father or grandfather, was still assumed over the household. However, the family was generally smaller. It usually included the husband, wife, and children plus one or two grandparents, an aunt or uncle or two, and perhaps other relatives. This size and style of family life worked well in the beginning days of industrialization and urbanization. But the development of changed patterns of work and living also paved the way for the next style of family, *the modern democratic family.* Characteristics of this style of family are:

(1) freedom of choice of a mate on the basis of romance, companionship, compatibility, and common interests; (2) independence from their parents of the young people after marriage; (3) the assumption of equality of husband and wife; (4) decisions reached by discussion between husband and wife in which children participate increasingly with advancing age; and (5) the maximum of freedom for its members consistent with the achieving of family objectives.[3]

It is this modern democratic or companionship family which Burgess and Locke describe as the one emerging in contemporary society.

We must recognize immediately that each of these descriptions of family types is a model of something which does not exist completely in real-life situations. Most families are a blend of characteristics found in the patriarchal and the companionship types of relationships. Research studies by other sociologists and psychologists have shown this to be true.

For example, several studies of the general patterns of marital relations demonstrate that the modern companionship style has not replaced the traditional style among all of the persons interviewed.[4] Mirra Komanovsky described some of the men in her study as having "modified traditional" views of women in marriage. This means that women who desire to work should also plan to bear children and do the major housekeeping chores but with some assistance from her husband. Helena Z. Lopata found that women are more apt to favor equality and companionship roles in marriage while others have found men to be more traditional. The major contributing factor to reducing the patriarchal or male dominant stance for men is likely to be more extensive education.

Roper and Labeff concur with Burgess and Locke that men and women tend to favor greater equality for women in our modern world. However, they did not find as much support for equality in domestic roles as they did in political and economic roles. Men tended to be more traditional in defining the role of women in the home. Thus we must acknowledge the fact that contemporary marriage patterns reflect many different combinations of role expectations and behavior.

Another factor in society which affects the status of family life today is the crisis of the family itself. With over a million families being dissolved each year since 1976 by divorce, desertion, or annulment and with more adults living together without marriage, the condition of the family is seriously disturbed in our society. Dr. Urie Bronfenbrenner, a noted child-development expert, declared bluntly, "The family is falling apart."[5] He with other family-life specialists argue for a new priority to be given to family development in our society. Certainly we would all agree with that call for renewal in family emphasis.

One of the problems for us, though, is the belief that simply returning to an older style of family development will solve these difficulties. Burgess and Locke were prophetic about our own day when they declared, "At a time of social crisis one disposition on the part of the public is to advocate the presentation of the traditional form of organization or a return to it."[6] Much of the literature interpreting Christian marriage prescribes return to patriarchal marital styles as the only way to achieve stable family relations in contemporary marriage. In order to evaluate what Christians can do to improve marriage and family living, let us examine some of the books offering recommendations for successful family living.

Models of Marital Relationships

We have already suggested that marriage styles form a continuum from traditional or institutional to companionship or partnership. This continuum can be visualized as a line from one to the other.

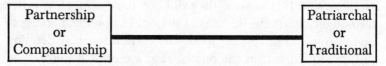

Partnership or Companionship		Patriarchal or Traditional

Some of the popular books maintain that marriages must be at the traditional end of the continuum to be considered Christian. Other authors affirm the necessity of being at the companionship end if the marriage is to be Christian. As we survey some representatives of each view, it is important to accept the Christian integrity of each author. Our purpose is not to judge the Christian character of the writers but to consider their teachings against the background of our discussion of equality and submission in marriage.

Traditional marriage and family relationships. David and

Vera Mace, in their book *We Can Have Better Marriages If We Really Want Them,* provide a definition of traditional marriage which reflects the earlier work of Burgess and Locke. They point out that in the traditional marriage "all relationships between men and women were hierarchically structured. A man's role in marriage was to be the head, to take charge, to issue orders, and to make decisions. A woman's role was to do what she was told, to treat her husband with respect even when she didn't agree with him, to suppress her feelings of hostility and resentment in order to keep the peace."[7]

It is this model of family life that is presented by a number of contemporary writers as the only authentically Christian way of relating in the family. For example in *How to Be Happy Though Married,* Tim LaHaye maintains that the traditional pattern of the family is the only one that can provide happiness. He declares that "one of the great hindrances to a happy home today is the false notion that a woman does not have to subject herself to her husband . . . . But when subjection goes out of the home, so does happiness."[8]

LaHaye seems to see only two alternatives in family relationships; male-dominance or female-dominance. In his view, male-dominance is right because:

God intended man to be the head of his house. If he is not, he will not have a sense of responsibility but will subconsciously feel he is married to a second mother. His children will soon detect who is boss, and as teenagers they will lose the natural respect for their father that is necessary for their adjustment to life.

He further maintains that the alternative is a wife-dominated, quarrelsome home in which the husband usually retreats from his rightful place of headship. According to LaHaye, the Christian response of a woman can only be "by faith to accept the fact that submission to her husband is for a woman's good.

Another popular guidebook on Christian relationships in the home is *The Christian Family* by Larry Christenson. Basing his approach to the divine order for family life on 1 Corinthians

11:3 and Colossians 3:20, Christenson describes the family structure as a hierarchy of authority:

The husband lives under the authority of Christ and is responsible to Christ for the leadership and care of the family. The wife lives under the authority of her husband and is responsible to him for the way she orders the household and cares for the children. The children live under the authority of both parents. The authority over the children, however remains essentially one since the authority of the mother is a derived authority. She exercises authority over the children on behalf of and in place of her husband.[9]

Christenson emphatically believes that "God has structured the family along clear-cut lines of authority and responsibility" and "any change from that which his will has ordered only brings forth a misshapen form, for which there is no cure except a return to God's original order."

This popular Lutheran pastor and writer is grounded in the Lutheran approach to social institutions as "orders of creation" through which God regulates human affairs. His approach to marriage gives explicit support to the adoption of social and economic roles based upon male/female distinctions. For example, he maintains that "the burden of caring for the support of the family lies upon the man" since the burden is too heavy for the woman.

Stronger shoulders are given to the man; he has a greater natural strength of mind to enable him to stand up under the pressure of these cares . . . . Therefore, also, he (God) has spared her the responsibility for supporting her family.[10]

Christenson does place an equal responsibility on the husband and wife to live in the continuing presence of Christ's lordship in the home, and his book has been studied by many families. However, in his rigid role theory and proof-text method of using Scripture, he fails to allow room for any other model of family relationships in Christian marriage than the traditional one. He fails, it seems to me, to allow the believer to live in the freedom of the Spirit who gives guidance to different ways of relating even though he is strongly supportive to God's Spirit working in the home.

In Jack Taylor's *One Home Under God*, a very helpful word is spoken on the importance of mutual submission in marital happiness as he and his wife experienced revival in their marriage. His overall plan for marriage, however, reflects the traditional emphasis on a hierarchy of authority. Taylor declares that "no organization can function properly without submission. Submission suggests authority. The whole of nature operates on authority and submission. To take these factors away would be to destroy the whole realm of nature."[11]

In his discussion of the wife's submission to her husband, Taylor does introduce more complementarity to the relationship than the other authors whom we have mentioned. However, he is just as firm in his position that submission is divinely ordained.

God has ordered the wife to be submissive to her husband, that is to yield to his authority. This is her God-given role. God only gives good things . . . . Wife, don't try to figure out this matter of submission. Lead with your heart and receive the capacity of submission as a perfect gift from God.

Taylor really strives to keep in balance the equality of persons in the Christian marriage which each share as partners and the authority structures which he considers necessary for marriage to survive. His exuberant proclamation of partnership is refreshing!

What a glorious partnership is shared in the marriage relationship! Here are partners who have submitted their lives to each other unconditionally and permanently. All that is faced will be faced *together*. What a wonderful word . . . together![12]

It would seem possible for such a partnership to overcome the necessity for maintaining such strict authority lines, but Taylor does not discuss how the partnership can function in shared authority.

In the Basic Youth Conflicts seminars, Bill Gothard also advocates a hierarchical model of family relationship in his emphasis on the chain-of-command authority structure. Bockelman in his evaluative book concerning Gothard, points out that "the chain of command means that everyone is under authority, and God deals with people through these channels of authority. God, of course, is the chief authority, and He works through four basic structures: family, government, church and business."[13]

The father is at the head of the chain of command for the family with the mother next and the children last. As Bockelman indicates, Gothard defines authority in terms of protection rather than domination. It is the umbrella of protection which the husband is to provide for the wife and children. Gothard says, "Authority is like an *'umbrella for protection'* and when we get out from under it, we expose ourselves to unnecessary temptations which are too strong for us to overcome."[14]

The most startling conclusion that Gothard advances is that the judgment on the wife recorded in Genesis 3 not only subjects her to her husband but also provides in some way for her husband's umbrella of protection to shield her from Satan. This seems to me to violate completely the individual, personal accountability for sin described by Paul in Romans 14:7–12. In addition, it appears to violate the individual's response to the direct influence of either the flesh or the Spirit in Galatians 5:16–25 and 6:7–8. There can be no equal responsibility for sin for both husband and wife if the husband and father can stand between his wife and children and the power of Satan in the world. This concept does honor the influence of a godly father as he provides an example of Christian living to his family, but it goes beyond New Testament teachings about our individual accountability to Christ for sin and forgiveness.

The Gothard seminars have benefited many thousands of Christians because of his strong emphasis on the need for forgiveness in family relationships, as well as his skill in providing very practical guidance for establishing patterns of interaction in the family. However, in his demand for female submissiveness even to the point of enduring physical and emotional abuse from her husband, Gothard argues for a principle that sacrifices human dignity for the woman. It may also cause her death or disfigurement while she waits for her husband to be changed through her submissiveness. Gothard maintains that "in our day the source of most conflicts with authority is not over commands to do wrong actions but in demonstrations of wrong attitudes by those under authority." He describes these wrong attitudes as "ungratefulness, disrespect, disloyalty, and pride." With regard to the obedience of a Christian wife to her husband, Gothard declares that a "person should *never* do evil, even if asked to do so by one in authority." However, the wife "must have a spirit of obedience"[15] even if she refuses to do evil at her husband's command. The husband is authority to his wife and she must be submissive to that authority unless asked to do evil by him.

It seems to me that the perversity of human sin is not sufficiently recognized in this command for obedience to male domination. To this degree his approach can and does induce anger and resentment in many women who believe he declares God's final word for their marriages.

Another of the popular advocates of female submissiveness is Marabel Morgan in *The Total Woman* (and *Total Joy*). Morgan declares emphatically that "it is only when a woman surrenders her life to her husband, reveres and worships him, and is willing to serve him, that she becomes really beautiful to him." Through such submission she becomes his queen and "a queen shall not nag or buck her king's decision after it is decreed." Since this type of family structure is the only one ordained by God, "there is no way you can alter or improve this relationship."[16]

One of the major criticisms of *The Total Woman* is that sex is prescribed as a manipulative device to entice a husband into fulfilling the wife's own desires or needs. Morgan explicitly rejects this idea in a sentence that also depreciates women as a group. She says, "Don't use sex as a weapon or a reward . . . . God understood women. He knew they would probably use the prized possession of sex to manipulate men, and He warned against rationing it out." In spite of this admonition against using sexual responsiveness manipulatively, Morgan does declare that if the total woman surrenders to her husband's way, "he in turn will gratefully respond by trying to make up to her and grant her desires."[17] Her book does encourage the exercise of power by submissiveness which can be used manipulatively by women in marriage to control the relationship.

Perhaps, however, the underlying view of man as so egocentric that he must always be buttered up or flattered is the most subtle blow against equality of personhood. The total woman is really a superior person who caters to the poor husband's needs in order to make him feel good. This concept of what a man is may be true in many marriages, but it need not be so in an authentically Christian one.

Each of these approaches to Christian marriage focuses on the necessity of submission and emphasizes its importance to fulfillment in marriage. The problem is that the responsibility for submission is placed totally on the wife with little attention being given to the mutual yieldedness in love which we have described in previous chapters. In addition, the male-dominant style is declared to be the only pattern of relationship which can be called Christian. Therefore, that style must be prescribed for all marriages. These authors fail to give attention to successful Christian marriages which are following the pattern of partnership rather than traditional relationships and do not acquaint their readers with other options for adjustment. This failure, of course, is because these authors are convinced that traditional marriage is the only truly Christian style. But is this true? Are there not Christian marriages which successfully live a partnership style of relationship? In order to answer this question, let us review the writings of some of the authors who describe marriage as companionship or partnership.

Companionship marriage and family relationships. The Maces define a companionship marriage as "one which makes the man and woman equal partners." They point out that "at the heart of the new companionship marriages lies the desire of both partners for intimacy, closeness, and the deep sharing of life experiences."[18]

In the partnership or companionship model, each person is accepted as having equal worth in God's redemptive love, and this gives them equal status in the family relationship which they each help to create. Equality in this sense does not mean sameness; instead, it means that the differences between man and woman are recognized and honored in the particular way that a couple work out their own role fulfillment with each other. It is obvious that every marriage must establish some kind of role definition in order to function. The partnership style gives each partner equal voice in determining what the role relationship will be. Samuel Southard expresses concisely the basic assumptions of this approach when he says, "The old marital assumptions were ownership of the mate and denial of the self. The new culture stresses equality for the female and self-actualization of both partners."[19]

Dr. and Mrs. David Mace are internationally known family educators and counselors. Before coming to the United States to live and work, they were the developers of the National Marriage Guidance Council in England. For several years they were joint executive directors of the American Association of Marriage Counselors and are most recently the founders of the Association of Couples for Marriage Enrichment (ACME). By experience in marriage and work the Maces live and teach the partnership style of Christian marriage.

In *We Can Have Better Marriages If We Really Want Them*, the Maces describe some of the alternate styles of living together which have emerged in our own time as part of the rejection of marriage. They point back to the affirmation of Burgess and Locke that the companionship marriage was beginning to replace the authoritarian model and then ask, "What went wrong?" Why do many critics of marriage give little attention to the possibility of creating companionship marriages?

Their conclusion is that "the concept of the companionship marriage *did* emerge" and "*many* American marriages today are living demonstrations of that ideal." These marriages are "dedicated to a fully equalitarian acceptance of each other." But they are also quite aware that many marriages do not function as a companionship. This may be because of the belief that the dominant-submissive pattern is the only acceptable one or because couples discover that the "transition from the traditional marriage to the companionship marriage is far from easy."[20] It includes a new set of values and new approaches to role fulfillment. Decision making requires more communication and more willingness to consider the mates' point of view. Thus too many couples who tried to become partners ended up as adversaries. This failure to achieve their goal was primarily because they had neither models nor teaching to help them make the transition. The Maces describe marriage-enrichment programs and family-life education as fundamental needs for continuing to lead more couples into companionship marriages. "The development of a really good marriage is not a natural process," maintain the Maces, "it is an achievement."[21]

The ACME organization was developed to give national attention to this challenge for helping couples commit themselves to marital growth in acceptance and mutual fulfillment.

Like the One You Love, by Samuel Southard, is subtitled *Intimacy and Equality in Modern Marriage* and is thus identified as a discussion of marriage as a partnership of equals. Southard is a former professor of pastoral care at Southern Baptist Theological Seminary in Louisville, Kentucky, who became director of professional services and coordinator of training at the Georgia Mental Health Institute. He is now a pastor.

After reviewing some of the books and articles which are either critical or rejecting of marriage in today's society, Southard introduces his own approach.

A plan for new life-styles must balance commitment to a mate with fulfillment of the self. More specifically, there must be equality of the sexes. Men and women must be intimate friends who find in each other the qualities they enjoy in themselves. Mutual admiration is mixed with sexual affection and social responsibility. The result is a formula: Like the one you love.[22]

In order to have this kind of marriage, each partner must have a happy sense of personhood. Women as well as men must experience the joy of self-possession in which giving oneself is a voluntary act of love rather than a demand to be fulfilled. Southard also concurs with the Maces that "the principles of companionship marriage are for people who can grow."[23]

His chapter entitled "Share Without Surrender" is a clear description of his emphasis on equality. Southard recognizes that many men and women enter marriage with exceedingly high expectations for emotional fulfillment. These needs can make demands that literally consume the other person and can also be the basis for dissatisfaction with one's mate after marriage. Sharing without surrender is based upon a realistic appraisal of individual capacities to give to the other which becomes the foundation for intimacy in the marriage. One partner cannot assume that the other will meet every felt need, but each learns how to give emotionally, physically, and spiritually to the other in a yieldedness that is not the surrender of personhood. As Southard expresses it, this is to treat one's mate as a friend as well as a lover.

Jean Stapleton and Richard Bright are wife and husband who married after being widowed in their first marriages. Richard had been in campus ministries for twenty years before becoming a marriage and family counselor. Jean is head of the Journalism Department at East Los Angeles College. At the time of their marriage in 1973, they decided that Jean would retain her maiden name as a symbol of their shared emphasis on equality. They recognize that this is not essential to creating a partnership marriage but was a personal decision for their own relationship.

The authors set the purpose of their book against the backdrop of the many volumes written on women's liberation, antimarriage, or against shared intimacy in marriage. They point out that their book is not one of these but is one discussing "how to live as equals in a marriage and reap the reward of not only having greater personal fulfillment but also of having a better marriage."[24]

Equal marriage, as they describe it, is a form of companionship marriage. As such it is distinct from the traditional marriage we have described earlier in the chapter. The authors are convinced that traditional marriage patterns as taught in *Total Woman* and *Fascinating Womanhood* will work since power relationships are clearly defined, but true intimacy cannot grow in such marriages because of the inequality between the mates. But equal marriage is also different from the *Open Marriage* concept of George and Nena O'Neill. *Open Marriage* possesses many of the characteristics of equal marriage, but "it differs from equal marriage in that it lacks commitment and intimacy." Equal marriage is an approach that is centered between these two extremes. Their conclusion is that "marriages of the future will be commitments of two equals to each other, that intimacy will be increasingly the goal toward which couples strive in their marriages."[25]

Their discussion of "Who's the Boss?" is an excellent commentary on equality in marital decision making. They point out that in the traditional marriage, major decisions are often made by one person, usually the man. In equal marriages, two approaches are possible: "They may either make all important decisions jointly, or they may designate some decisions as those to be made by the husband and an equal group of decisions as those to be made by the wife." While they believe true intimacy grows best with joint decision making, couples may choose to make decisions on the basis of competence or function rather than jointly. In either event, equal decision making requires compromise which involves "having respect for each other and not questioning each other's basic integrity."[26]

Out of their own experience in working to create equal marriages in their first marriages as well as in their present relationship, Stapleton and Bright are convinced that "an equal intimate marriage will not lead to loss of freedom and stifling of growth but to different freedoms and a new potential for growth."[27]

Building a Better Marriage is one of a series of booklets on family enrichment produced by the Family Ministry Department of The Sunday School Board of the Southern Baptist Convention. Author Reuben Herring writes from the perspective of companionship marriage with an emphasis on changing role relations from rigid to flexible in modern marriage. He assumes that "Paul definitely preached the equality of men and women in Christ," thus "before a man becomes a husband and a woman becomes a wife, each is a person." The primary goal of marriage is "to help each partner to fulfill himself as a person."[28] The growth exercises described in the booklet are designed to help couples improve the partnership of marriage.

Now that we have sampled the writings of several authors committed to the companionship model of marriage, let us summarize some fundamental implications of this approach to Christian marriage.

First, each person in the marriage is directly responsible to Christ in personal faith and responsibility in a way that cannot be mediated by another person. The first great commandment of the Christian faith is affirmed by Jesus when he told an enquiring lawyer, "You shall love the Lord your God with all your heart, and with all your soul, and with all your mind"

(Matt. 22:37). Peter and the other apostles in Acts affirmed one's primary loyalty to God when they told the Sanhedrin, "We must obey God rather than men" (5:29). Paul reminded the Roman believers that they must honor each other's convictions because in the final analysis each person is directly responsible to Christ as Lord and "each of us shall give account of himself to God" (Rom. 14:12). It is by the armor of God's Holy Spirit, not by the umbrella of the husband's faith, that a woman, a young person, or any person is able to "stand against the wiles of the devil" (Eph. 6:11).

Second, male/female distinctions are not made the fundamental basis for differing structures of authority even though role distinctions can be and are made on the basis of male/female roles the couple work out for themselves.

The equality of the sexes in the accepting grace of God as affirmed by Paul in Galatians 3:28 is foundational to the companionship model. Submission is a mutual response to grace and in that submission to one another the couple are free to work out their relationship to one another in a manner best suited to their own personalities and competencies.

Third, parents are equally responsible for the guidance of children and equally worthy of honor from the children.

As far back as the Ten Commandments, the biblical faith demands equal responsibility to father and mother in the Fifth Commandment: "Honor your father and your mother, that your days may be long in the land which the Lord your God gives you" (Ex. 20:12). This Commandment is reaffirmed by Paul when he said, "Children, obey your parents in the Lord, for this is right" (Eph. 6:1). In these passages no hierarchy of responsibility is described. The child is directly responsible to both parents, and the mother does not exercise an authority over the children derived from the father. They are her children as well as his, and she is to exercise her own authority over them.

Fourth, decision making is accomplished through mutual dis-

cussion and the willingness to practice the love described in
1 Corinthians which "does not insist on its own way" (1 Cor.
13:5). Decisions must be made in all marriages, obviously, and
are worked out by the couple in a manner that gives equal
involvement in the decision-making process to both husband
and wife.

Fifth, the companionship model presents more possibility
for conflict since role relationships are not structured on sexual
roles but must be worked out in love with each other.

The Clinebells provide an excellent discussion of this aspect
of companionship marriage in *The Intimate Marriage*:

Modern marriage, with its robust emphasis on companionship, communication, and equality, offers unprecedented possibilities for the
growth of depth relationships. But the democratic model of marriage
also offers more opportunities for conflict and progressive alienation.
It puts more demands on the partners than did the older patriarchal
model. Roles are changing rapidly and in ways that are threatening
to husbands and to wives. The increased communication, mutual sharing, and openness which are at the heart of the new model mean
that both partners are asked to give more of themselves to the relationship . . . . Such are the dilemmas and the challenge of modern marriage. The same factors—openness, equality, communication, companionship—which create new potentialities for conflict also present us
with the opportunity to develop relationships of unprecedented depth
and mutual fulfillment.[29]

It must not be assumed, therefore, that conflict in itself is
sinful or necessarily destructive to marriage and family relationships. Conflict is an experience which the Bible records over
and over again in the lives of the people of God. It is minimized
when one person makes all decisions and magnified when decisions must be made by two or more persons, but it can be a
healthy part of creating mutual satisfaction through the decision-making process.

The Maces identify marital conflict as "a disagreement, a
state of opposed wills, that has been *heated up by emotion*—
anger, resentment, hurt, feelings, anxiety. The emotion is

caused by frustration because you want or need something
and you can't get it." Many marriage counselors would agree
with their conviction that harmonious marital relationships are
dependent on "whether or not the couple learn the process
of mutual adjustment that enables them to resolve their differences and to enter into a close and intimate interpersonal relationship. In other words, learning the process is the key that
opens the door to the companionship marriage."[30] Dr. James
Flamming, pastor of the First Baptist Church, Abilene, Texas,
spoke pointedly to this issue at the Glorieta Baptist Conference
Center when he said, "It is impossible to be intimate with
someone with whom you have not been emotional. Anger can
certainly be emotional!"

Paul's word to the Ephesian Christians concerning the han-
dling of anger is particularly relevant to this discussion. In
Ephesians 4:26–27, Paul said, "Be angry but do not sin; do
not let the sun go down on your anger, and give no opportunity
to the devil." The passage includes an explicit awareness that
anger does develop between believers, that anger is to be recognized and expressed in some fashion. But the Christian must
be careful not to let anger become sinful by being suppressed
into one's personality where it can become resentment and
hostility. Anger between Christian mates must be acknowledged and worked through before it becomes destructive to
the relationship. So Paul said that we should not allow anger
to build up overnight since this might give opportunity for
sin to develop. Hostile, angry feelings must be acknowledged,
named for what they are, and overcome in the relationship.

In contrast, Paul commanded Christian fathers, "Do not provoke your children to anger, but bring them up in the discipline
and instruction of the Lord" (Eph. 6:4). In this case, the anger
against which Paul warned is the internalized resentment or
wrath that is destructive to the parent-child relationship. Parents and children are normally going to have times when they
are angry with each other, but this anger must not be allowed

to become wrath or resentment. The differences must be resolved and love allowed to prevail in such a way that forgiveness
is both given and received from each participant in the conflict.
Through such a process of recognition of anger, resolution of
the causes of anger, and reconciliation between the family
members the fullest meaning of intimacy and grace is encouraged to grow.

The last implication of this model which I would emphasize
is its implicit dependence upon the continuing presence of
the Holy Spirit in his work of teaching, guiding, and strengthen-
ing the Christian couple in their marriage relationship.

Jesus declared that the Holy Spirit would be the Christian's
Counselor in teaching all things (John 14:25–26), and Paul
maintained that "the Lord is the Spirit, and where the Spirit
of the Lord is, there is freedom" (2 Cor. 3:17). The fruit of
the Spirit in the believer's life is love, joy, peace, patience,
kindness, goodness, faithfulness, gentleness, and self-control
(Gal. 5:22). These are all essential qualities of the companionship marriage if it is to be successful.

In this dependence upon the Holy Spirit, couples have an
opportunity to work out their own place on the spectrum of
marriage that stretches from traditional to companionship. Under God, the couple can allow their love for one another and
their response to the cultural patterns of marriage to determine
how their own Christian family life will function.

Samuel Southard has a good word for us when he points
out that:

If a custom cradles some truth in which they believe, it should be
respected. But as social arbiters press for some conformity that is
not true to the marriage relationship, the couple can remind their
anxious friends that the customs of marriage are changing. The traditional ways may benefit some, but there are new ways to self-acceptance after a wedding ceremony.[31]

In conclusion, therefore, I would affirm the conviction that
couples who love each other in the fullest sense of Christian

love and who are committed to Christ's leadership in their lives can work out any one of a number of modifications of these patterns of relationship and find happiness. Sensitivity to the Lord's will for their individual lives and willingness to be open to each other in investigating their own understandings of marriage can lead them to fulfilling relationships.

Choosing Your Own Marriage Pattern

Couples usually relate to one another in one of four types of relationships. One type is the independent-independent relationship in which each person maintains his own identity and there is little depth sharing of commitments. *Open Marriage* tends to encourage this kind of relationship. A second type is the independent-dependent relationship in which one partner exercises the dominant role and the other is submissive. If the male is dominant, this type is what we have called the traditional style of relationship.

A third possible type is the dependent-dependent relationship with both partners having a clinging need for each other which may keep them married even if the needs become neurotic and destructive. The fourth type is that of mutual interdependence. In this marriage relationship the partners are permitted to be equal individuals but with strongly felt needs for each other which are expressed in mutual sharing of intimacy. This pattern is demonstrated in the companionship model.

How a given couple form their own relationship will be influenced by parental models, personality and temperament characteristics, religious teachings and personal experience. At times a relationship based upon personality needs will be defended on theological grounds if the couple are not aware that the personality influence is so great. For example, a woman whose great need for dependent relationships with a man was shaped by her relationship to her father may become an ardent defender of women's submission in marriage because it meets her emotional need. She may be unwilling to acknowledge that other women have personality styles more adapted to mutual interdependence and that they have a Christian right to develop their marriage on that pattern.

Generally couples establish their pattern of relating during the first eighteen months of marriage. Many couples will continue to live out the style of relationship they found satisfactory in those early months because it meets their dependency needs. If the relationship has been formed on the independent-dependent style but has retained the essential characteristics of love and respect, the couple can be very happy in their marriage. As Southard suggests, "Many adequate persons are happy with traditional ties. They like their roles as husband and wife, which have come down, with slight alteration only, through the centuries."[32] This marriage pattern is toward the right end of the marital spectrum.

If the relationship has been formed on a mutually interdependent style with full affirmation of the equality of mates in status and role definition, it will be at the left of the spectrum.

But many marriages will result in a blending of these styles in such a way that they will not be fully traditional or fully companionship. If a wife desires to be treated with respect as an equal person in the marriage but still wants her husband to take a more dominant role in family headship, that marriage pattern will be slightly to the left or right of center. Its actual position will be subject to some fluctuation based on differing role expectations.

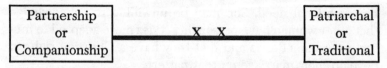

Partnership or Companionship	X X	Patriarchal or Traditional

The important consideration here is that this marriage is also Christian. Under the guidance of the Holy Spirit and in their commitment to building a Christian marriage, couples are free to work out role relationships which meet their own personality needs.

If your goal is to create more of a companionship union after having lived in a traditional marriage, this choice is definitely yours to make. If you need a more structured form of relationship based on traditional styles, this, too, is an authentic Christian choice. However, the transition from traditional to companionship requires willingness to grow in understanding, in communication, in self-assurance, and in grace. Change in any system of interaction between persons tends to occur slowly and unevenly. One partner may change more rapidly than the other.

Arlene Silberman is exactly right in her comment on changing roles: "The times they are a-changing, but traditional husbands can't give up traditional habits cold-turkey. Neither can traditional wives, even those who say they want to."[33] Her article is addressed to women, but its wisdom can apply to both men and women in changing marriages, especially in her final bit of advice: "For a woman [man] to become liberated, the man [woman] and the marriage must also be liberated. Marriages that are made in heaven must be worked out on earth." With patience and persistence, it is possible to move from institution to companionship when husband and wife each desire such a change.

Let me share with you the story of one couple who decided to do so. Kay and Kent live in Springfield, Massachusetts, but Kay's story was written for friends in Kansas City. She gave permission to use it in the hope that it might be helpful to other couples desiring to grow a partnership marriage.

All my life I wanted to be married. From the time I was in kindergarten I was positive that my boyfriend of the moment, whether he knew it or not, was the one I would marry. My idea of marriage was, of course, juvenile and romantic and unrealistic. Not having a close relationship with my father, I was seeking for total security and male attention, and felt sure that marriage would provide these.

When, at age 21, I actually was married, I was in reality as much in need of a father as a husband. Having become a follower of Christ in my teens, I was determined to be a Christian wife, and in my mind that meant one word—support. To support my husband in whatever he chose to do, to do whatever he asked of me as well as I could, to create a serene atmosphere in which he could develop as a man of God, to be hospitable to his friends, etc., etc., but above all, NEVER to argue. An admirable example of wifely submission, you might say. And so it went—he went about the business of being God's man, and I tried to cooperate with all his plans.

Then, one day, came a disturbing incident. He asked my opinion about something and I gave my usual response, "Whatever you think, Honey." And . . . he got *mad!* It seemed that he wanted and had been wanting all this time, my honest participation in thinking something through with him, and I resisted doing that because I wanted him to bear *all* the responsibility. My concept of submission and a peaceful home had been wrong—it had been a total cop-out for me. My husband did want my support; but more than this, he wanted a partner who would share the responsibility for the decisions that needed to be made.

As you might imagine, this situation couldn't change over night. In fact, I'm still struggling with the challenges of becoming a partner. Both of us have learned a few things in this adventure called marriage and are conscious that there is much to learn.

The first thing to be recognized and dealt with was my well-hidden but very real spirit of competition with him. It was feeling inferior that kept me from being a partner. After all, he was so much better and stronger and more disciplined than I, what could I have to offer a partnership? But God said "the two shall become one flesh," and I have come to discover that this implies being thankful for my deficiencies because they can be filled by another's sufficiency. The marriage is an experience of the body of Christ in which each member needs the other. Each of us has been supplied with something the other lacks, and I have begun to learn that rather than bemoan my deficiencies, I can rejoice that my partner is strong where I am weak, and he can discover in me strengths I didn't know I had. This realization can enable us to share our weaknesses, even our garbage, with each other because we are not in a goodness contest.

And we have begun to learn that we can call out each other's gifts—that we can see qualities in each other because of our intimacy that others can't readily see, and we can encourage the development of these. The recognition of gifts plus the greater sense of being together frees us to sometimes step out of our roles. It's no longer inappropriate for Kent to prepare a school-morning breakfast, nor is it inappropriate for me to recalk the bathtub.

We have learned that married people can minister to each other better than anyone else—we are uniquely qualified to see what each other needs. The difficulty is allowing this mutual ministry to take place, because it means trusting each other to deal with our weaknesses gently and not use them against each other.

And finally we are enabled to minister to others together in a way that continually surprises us—because we complement and modify each other and each of us sees different aspects of a problem others might have, our pooled perspectives allow us to be more help to another couple or individual than we could be alone.

As to the mechanics of how the partnership works, it's best seen, I think, in our decision-making processes, whether this is planning our calendar for the next six months or deciding what to pray for our children. The calendar has been a real point of tension for us. A major part of shifting from supporter to partner is, for me, becoming willing to struggle with the planning of our time. I used to be in a dilemma about this—I hated planning future involvements because it was so overwhelming I didn't want to think about it, which left Kent in the position of having to do the planning alone. Then, when the various commitments had to be honored, I would be resentful because they were his commitments, not ours. Obviously, I couldn't have it both ways, so now we periodically sit down with our calendar and submit to each other all our ideas and desires, and we don't do anything unless we *both* feel right about it.

The most obvious benefit in making decisions together is the freedom from guilt about our individual involvements. Because we decided together that I would serve on a board of the church, I don't need to feel guilty about the time spent in board meetings; because we decide together what trips Kent will take, he doesn't need to feel guilty about being away from home. In fact, we experience a real sense of each others' spiritual presence in our individual involvements because of having spent the time it took to come to agreement on these things.

Our prayer life has been revolutionized too. We are trying to operate on the principle of "agreement" as set forth in Matthew 18:19, where Jesus said, "If two of you shall agree about anything, . . . it will be done . . . by my Father." Agreement is hard work; it does *not* mean capitulation—and I am a very experienced capitulator. Not capitulating sometimes means doing something I formerly abhorred and feared—arguing. But there is a difference between destructive and constructive arguing. Destructive arguing is full of despair and constructive arguing is full of hope. The hope comes from the knowledge that we will keep working on an issue until it is resolved. Our procedure is to set aside certain periods of time during which we think and talk together about out desires for various people and situations until we feel we have a handle on what God wants to do about it, and that becomes our prayer. It is sometimes easy to do this and sometimes hard to come to agreement, but it has the result of bringing us together on the important issues of our lives and enables us to discover the mind of the Lord concerning the things we care about.

Sometimes I think there is no more demanding relationship on earth than the marriage relationship, but it is never boring. A few years ago I felt momentary panic when I thought maybe we had experienced all there was—that we had plateaued. But almost immediately there were more mountains in front of us. The process of two people finding out what it is to become one is never finished, but then no one wants to be finished with something that's fun.

Amen and Amen!

Notes

1. Ernest W. Burgess and Harvey J. Locke, *The Family: From Institution to Companionship* (New York: American Book Co., 1945), p. vii.

2. Ibid., p. 18.

3. Ibid., pp. 21–22.

4. Brent S. Roper and Emily Labeff, "Sex Roles and Feminism Revisited: An Intergenerational Attitude Comparison," *Journal of Marriage and the Family*, (February, 1977), pp. 113–119.

5. Urie Bronfenbrenner, "Nobody Home: The Erosion of the American Family," *Psychology Today* (May, 1977), p. 41.

6. Burgess and Locke, p. 714.

7. Mace, *We Can Have Better Marriages*, p. 74.

8. Tim LaHaye, *How to Be Happy Though Married* (Wheaton, Illinois: Tyndale House, 1968), pp. 105–108.

9. Larry Christenson, *The Christian Family* (Minneapolis: Bethany Press, 1970), p. 18.

10. Ibid., pp. 127–128.

11. Jack Taylor, *One Home Under God* (Nashville: Broadman Press, 1974), pp. 24–39.

12. Ibid., p. 58.

13. Wilfred Bockelman, *Gothard—the Man and His Ministry: An Evaluation* (Santa Barbara: Twill Publications, 1976), p. 69.

14. Ibid., p. 73.

15. Joseph Bagley, "How Basic the Conflict: An Open Letter from Bill Gothard," *Eternity* (August, 1977), p. 41.

16. Marabel Morgan, *The Total Woman* (New York: Pocket Books, 1975), pp. 96–97, 82–84.

17. Ibid., pp. 138, 83.

18. Mace, p. 74.

19. Southard, *Like the One You Love*, p. 11.

20. Mace, p. 55.

21. Ibid., p. 111.

22. Southard, pp. 11–12.

23. Ibid., p. 31.

24. Stapleton and Bright, *Equal Marriage*, p. 8.

25. Ibid., pp. 19–20.

26. Ibid., pp. 45, 53.

27. Ibid., p. 132.

28. Reuben Herring, *Building a Better Marriage* (Nashville: Convention Press, 1975), pp. 9, 15.

29. Clinebell, *The Intimate Marriage*, pp. 19–20.

30. Mace, pp. 29–31.

31. Southard, p. 43.

32. Ibid., p. 14.

33. Arlene Silberman, "Can a Woman Become Liberated—and Stay Married?" *Readers Digest* (August, 1977), pp. 71–74.

Index

Authors and Subjects

Scripture References